A GIFT FOR

FROM

DATE

the
TRUST
JOURNEY

HEAL FROM BROKEN TRUST
WITH OTHERS, YOURSELF,
AND GOD

LYSA TERKEURST

THOMAS NELSON
Since 1798

The Trust Journey

Published in Nashville, Tennessee, by Thomas Nelson. Thomas Nelson is a registered trademark of HarperCollins Christian Publishing, Inc.

Photos by Hallie Worrell, Link Arms LLC.

Thomas Nelson titles may be purchased in bulk for educational, business, fund-raising, or sales promotional use. For information, please email SpecialMarkets@ThomasNelson.com.

Any internet addresses, phone numbers, or company or product information printed in this book are offered as a resource and are not intended in any way to be or to imply an endorsement by Thomas Nelson, nor does Thomas Nelson vouch for the existence, content, or services of these sites, phone numbers, companies, or products beyond the life of this book.

Interior design: Emily Ghattas

ISBN 978-1-4002-5082-0 (HC)
ISBN 978- (audiobook)
ISBN 978-1-4002-5083-7 (eBook)

Printed in Malaysia

25 26 27 28 29 COS 10 9 8 7 6 5 4 3 2 1

Contents

A Note from Lysa

Dear Friend,

Broken trust and betrayal are deeply hurtful experiences to walk through. In my own trust journey, I was so confused about how to heal and afraid to move forward. If you're holding this journal, it probably means you find yourself doubting others, yourself, and God. And you're not sure what to do now.

I wrote *I Want to Trust You, but I Don't* for these reasons. I realized the hurt of broken trust had affected me so deeply that it was starting to turn me into someone I didn't recognize. I found it hard to trust people—even people who hadn't broken my heart. Skepticism about some people was necessary, but I didn't want to get cynical about all people.

Also, I couldn't make sense of how a good God sometimes allows really heartbreaking realities to happen. So much felt confusing and unfair. And I'd lost so much of my carefree nature and confidence in my own discernment that it left me paralyzed.

A big motivation for my writing this journal was that I couldn't fit all the processing questions that I wanted us both to work on in the pages of the book. This message is designed to be worked through—not just quickly read. And I didn't want you to have to process all of this alone. So each day when you pick up this journal, you'll find me right there guiding and encouraging you. Plus, I've added additional content that isn't in the book. As I continued my journey, there was more I wanted to share from my heart to yours.

Maybe you've experienced small breaches of trust and want to work on these issues to make a current relationship stronger, or you've experienced a betrayal that has fractured a relationship, leaving it beyond repair. This journey will give us a better understanding of trust and some tools to help guide us biblically and therapeutically toward healthier trust practices. This journey will lead us forward in healing and learning to trust again.

Lastly, I am inspired by beautiful pictures. So I filled this journal with scenes of peace, serenity, and reminders that God is so very good and so completely trustworthy.

I'm so glad you're here.

Lysa

How to Use This Journal

This journal is intended to be used with the book *I Want to Trust You, but I Don't: Moving Forward When You're Skeptical of Others, Afraid of What God Will Allow, and Doubtful of Your Own Discernment*. Here I'll guide you in digging deeper into what we are reading in each chapter of the book.

You can write in complete sentences or list form. Don't worry about your sloppy handwriting, misspellings, or tears dropped on the page. You can answer all the chapter's questions in one sitting, or you can spread out your journaling, choosing a few questions to respond to each day.

You can skip questions, but I encourage you to come back to them. Sometimes the most challenging prompts will be just what you need for healing.

The message of this book about trust issues is not a one-and-done process. I want you to come back again as you feel the need to explore questions about trust. I hope that by the end of this book you feel better equipped with healthy tools to deal with trust issues that arise. It's designed for your quiet reflection, but it also can be a tool you use with a friend as you grow together in your trust journey.

Each chapter of *The Trust Journey* includes:

- **Fresh insights and highlights of main points.** You'll see new stories and insights, as well as quotations and summaries of thoughts from the chapter.
- **Guided journaling prompts and space to respond.** I'll ask you specific questions to help you reflect, process, write about, and implement what you're learning. Some questions will reference stories or point back to the book *I Want to Trust You, but I Don't*.
- **Action steps.** This is where we apply what we're learning by taking action steps to move forward. One ongoing step is to create a Moving Forward folder on your phone where you can collect images that remind you of trusting God, others, and yourself.
- **Scriptures.** You'll find scriptures taken from the chapter or related to the chapter. I encourage you to engage with these scriptures in many ways, even beyond your journaling here. You can write out the verses in different translations, be creative using colored pencils or highlighters, and work to memorize them.
- **Playlists.** I've included some of my favorite worship songs, chosen to accompany your journaling or for worship later. You'll notice most of the songs are contemporary, but I've also included more traditional hymns, in case you want to give those a try. You can also find songs on your own and add those to your playlist.
- **Guided prayers.** I've written short prayers to get you started in giving everything you're struggling with to God and have included space for you to write your own prayers.

Working Through Our Trust Issues Together

For years I have put labels on myself. Maybe I do it because a label can help me categorize or clarify the reasons I struggle with certain things.

For example, one of my labels is "I'm an introvert who is sometimes forced to live the life of an extrovert." People are usually surprised by this since I'm pretty comfortable speaking to crowds, and I can make easy conversation with people I meet. But put me in a social gathering with lots of surface conversations and, though I'm smiling on the outside, I feel terribly awkward on the inside.

Very quickly I start anticipating how soon I can regroup by myself. I'm a big fan of bathroom stalls for this reason. Though public restrooms aren't the loveliest places to recharge, I like the feeling of having my own private little space where I can shut the door, regroup, and be alone for a bit. Even if I don't really need to use the restroom, typically no one expects anything from you when you go there.

Another go-to label is "I'm directionally challenged." I have lived at the same address for more than thirty years. I have gone to the same hairdresser, the same hospital, the same shopping centers, and the same office for years. And I still use GPS directions just in case I get turned around. Last week I took a different exit to my office to save time. Though it's not the one I typically use, I have gone that way many, many times. And yet, I still got lost. And I had to have that awkward conversation with my team that the reason I was a few minutes late was because I got lost going between my house and the office . . . a route they know I've traveled for decades.

What are some of the labels you've placed on yourself that accurately portray some traits, quirks, funny habits, or even struggles you have?

Now let's think about the label "trust issues." Can you think of a situation where this label felt very appropriate to use about yourself or a challenging relationship?

_____

_____

_____

_____

_____

_____

_____

_____

_____

_____

_____

I don't shame myself for having introverted tendencies. I actually like having this label and the words I shared with you to inform people why alone time is important to me. I don't shame myself for being directionally challenged. I realize there are things I could do to get better at this, but I also don't mind accepting the help of the maps feature on my phone. But I'd like to admit something to you right up front.

I'm not nearly as compassionate toward myself with trust issues. If I'm with others who talk freely about their issues with trust, I feel safe enough to talk about mine. But if I'm in a situation where trust issues are spoken of like they're some sort of a bad smell or virus others don't want to catch, I feel this weird sense of shame. The shame plays out in one of two ways for me: either I get defensive and want to remind others that there are legitimate reasons I have trust issues, or I get quiet and make a note in my head that this person isn't someone I should be vulnerable with.

What part of this do you relate to?

_____

_____

_____

_____

_____

     In order to move forward we need to better understand where we've been and where we are.

Write about a childhood experience where someone that should have cared for you didn't. For some of us, this will be a traumatic event like abuse, abandonment, addiction, or being required to be the adult in a situation. For others, it will be something more subtle like belonging to a family where emotions weren't allowed to be expressed, issues were brushed under the rug to keep up appearances, or a parent was physically present but not nurturing like you needed them to be. Or maybe you were bullied by friends, ignored or shamed by teachers, or overlooked by loved ones. Briefly write about that here.

_____

_____

_____

_____

_____

_____

_____

_____

Here's the story I told myself about this event: (Before you answer, let's pause. Sometimes when a situation happens, we develop a narrative about others, God, or ourselves. Your journaling here will give you a chance to examine if this story is really true.)

_____

_____

_____

_____

_____

_____

_____

_____

How did this negatively impact your ability to trust those around you?

_____

_____

_____

_____

_____

_____

_____

_____

Now write about a more recent experience where you trusted someone, and that trust was broken. What happened? Why did you feel you could count on this person? Was the broken trust a slow erosion or a sudden event?

_____

_____

_____

_____

_____

_____

_____

_____

What story do you now tell yourself as a result of this situation?

_____

_____

_____

_____

_____

_____

_____

_____

_____

Are there any vows or promises you made to yourself in an effort to better protect your heart after the broken trust?

How do you think this may have impacted your ability to trust others in your life?

Are there any connections or commonalities between the broken trust of your childhood experience and the more recent experience with relationship betrayal?

_____

_____

_____

_____

_____

_____

_____

_____

_____

_____

Whew! You did it! You pushed through any discomfort surrounding journaling about trust issues. Maybe you sailed through those questions but you feel a bit unsure about what's to come. That's okay.

We'll take this one step at a time. This means we don't feel bad or shame ourselves for having trust issues. This is a safe place to be honest with ourselves and God. We don't move forward by ignoring or denying what's real. In fact, my counselor says that healthiness is a commitment to reality.

So let's be real. Let's be vulnerable. Yes, I know that can be hard. Yes, I know you might cry a little or a lot while you journal. I did. I do. But I can promise you that as I've walked this healing journey—and I'm still walking through it—I've found my way back to me, to the person I want to be. The person I know God wants me to be.

It's going to be worth every hard moment. We're doing this with one another and with God. I'm excited about the healing you, too, will find.

Fear Has the Louder Voice Right Now

I've had anxiety over many hard things in my life. But some of the most difficult situations are the ones where someone I thought I could count on broke my trust and my heart. You only have to be betrayed one time to start feeling angst and fear over the risks of relationships.

I remember being a young child on the playground at school, and a girl who I thought was my friend started making fun of me in front of the "cool kids." I'll never forget the feeling I had when she walked away with them, all laughing, and she didn't look back at me. I think that was the first time I realized sometimes people just want what they want, and if they hurt me in the process, they can justify it because it got them something they felt was worth more than their relationship with me. I'm not unique in this. We've all had our trust broken in various ways and to varying degrees.

But at some point we have to learn to walk forward in trust. In the process there will be fear because all human-to-human relationships carry with them the risk of getting hurt.

It's interesting that in the Bible the word for trustworthy is *batah*. When that word is used and directed toward God, it's always in a positive sense. But when that same word refers to human relationships, it almost always has a negative connotation, carrying with it the sense that people will not always be trustworthy. While we can always count on God, there will be times we can't trust others.

The trustworthy nature of God is certain.

Sometimes the trustworthy nature of others is not.

This doesn't mean that trust is impossible with others, but it does mean all relationships will need to be worked on with grace, wisdom, forgiveness, healthy boundaries, and an understanding of how trust does and does not work.

For much of my life, I didn't understand these relationship principles. But after studying and writing about most of these in my other books, I decided it was now time to tackle trust. More specifically, my issues with trust.

In a conversation after some hurtful situations, I told my friend Meredith that I didn't want to trust anyone ever again. The story I told myself was that relationships are just a recipe for eventual pain. I didn't want to experience that level of pain again; therefore, I thought the risks of trying to trust others were too high.

That's when she stopped me cold in my tracks with her reply: "Trust can only be repaired in the context of relationships. You can't repair it in isolation."

Of course, she didn't mean that I have to be in relationship with the one who hurt me over and over, but she did mean that I would have to risk some relationships in order to work on my issues with trust. I didn't like her answer very much. But I've come to understand it so much better now, and I realize she was right.

Here's the first thought I want you to consider as we get started. It comes from something my friend Dr. Joel Muddamalle said during a Q&A he and I hosted together. He was asked about getting over heartbreak and hurts and disappointments. He said, "One of the most powerful prepositions in the Bible is the word *through*."

The Israelites had to go *through* the Red Sea.

Jesus had to go *through* Samaria.

Jesus had to go *through* the suffering of the cross.

Sometimes we have to walk *through* stuff even when we desperately want to quickly get *over* it.

But going through is what will get us on the other side with a greater understanding that God has always and will always be with us.

On that note, let's work through the issues we have with trust—together.

Guided Journaling

Let's look at some main points from the introduction and respond to the guided prompts.

1. Reflect on the title and subtitle of the book: *I Want to Trust You, but I Don't: Moving Forward When You're Skeptical of Others, Afraid of What God Will Allow, and Doubtful of Your Own Discernment.* Do you think it's more challenging to trust others, God, or yourself? Why?

_____

_____

_____

_____

_____

_____

_____

_____

_____

_____

2. In the book's introduction, I wrote a number of "I want" statements. Which ones make you say, "Yes! That's what I want!"? Write some of your own "I want" statements. Think in terms of the categories of others, God, and self.

    For example:

    I want to believe I'll be safe with you.

    I want to believe in the goodness of God and that He really does care about what happens to me.

    I want to believe that I won't lie in bed sobbing over the red flags I missed or chose not to pay attention to.

    Write yours here:

    _____

    _____

    _____

    _____

    _____

3. Filtering everyone through my hurt was turning me into someone I'd never been before. I was so deeply affected by having my trust broken that I couldn't trust people close to me, and I started doubting myself and God. Can you, too, say that your reactions to the pain of broken trust have turned you into someone different? In what ways is this true of you? Maybe you've become bitter, vengeful, withdrawn, overly skeptical, isolated, stuck in victim mode, or cautious about forming new relationships. Is there anything about you right now that leads you to say, "This is not who I want to be"? Pray about this and see if there are places you can ask Jesus to help you change.

    _____

    _____

    _____

    _____

4. "But life kind of requires us to be trusting." What about this statement rings true to you? Write about what you'll miss out on if you don't trust others, God, or yourself. Can these things motivate you to move forward in trust?

_____

_____

_____

_____

_____

_____

5. The trauma of having your trust broken by people you thought would never betray you is life altering. But it doesn't have to be life ruining. Do you feel like broken trust has been life altering? Do you have the hope to believe it's not life ruining? Are there things you can start doing now to ensure that? What will help you right now to have a perspective shift?

_____

_____

_____

_____

_____

_____

_____

_____

_____

6. I got so tired of this weird dance so many of us do around the words "emotional abuse" that I decided to really dig into the physical damage that can be caused by emotional trauma. So I had my brain scanned by Dr. Amen, a physician and psychiatrist specializing in brain health.

The results of the brain scan showed that the emotional trauma I experienced had resulted in physical effects in an area in the brain called the "trauma diamond." Why was this so significant? Since there wasn't physical abuse—no bruises or broken bones—I sometimes found myself questioning the effects of the emotional trauma. *Am I overreacting? Am I being dramatic?* And others did the same thing when they minimized what I had gone through. Worse yet, I let their words fuel my distrust in myself.

Write about the effect of minimizing your own experiences. In what ways do you want to change when it comes to trusting yourself? Write about how others' disbelief has contributed to your trust issues.

7. Sometimes distrust is the most appropriate response. My issue with trusting certain people may honestly be a sign of wisdom, not weakness. My tendency to overanalyze their words and actions, or even a feeling I get when I'm around them, may actually be an exercise of discernment, not deficiency. Does this statement—"Sometimes distrust is the most appropriate response"—surprise you or affirm your thoughts? Write about situations where distrust was an appropriate response.

_____

_____

_____

_____

_____

_____

_____

_____

_____

_____

_____

_____

_____

_____

_____

_____

_____

8. In the introduction I share that I know the joy of moving into new seasons with fresh hope and better tools to attract and keep healthy relationships. I know the thrill of feeling safe enough to connect deeply with people who are trustworthy. I know how much courage it will take to keep walking into a future full of possibilities and risks worth taking. Which one of these thoughts can be a goal for you to move toward as you journal?

9. One more thing to remember throughout journaling: Let's be sure we don't think of this journaling process as something that will fix us. Yes, we'll address brokenness and healing. But broken is not my identity, and it's not yours.

    Have you labeled yourself as broken? Needing to be fixed? Has that become your identity? How can you shift your perspective about this? Does the idea that healing comes through focusing on God's love and staying close to Jesus change your perspective?

    _____

    _____

    _____

    _____

    _____

    _____

    _____

    _____

    _____

Action Steps

I often go through the camera roll on my phone to look for photos that represent my moving forward. I've found so many pictures of myself walking on paths, roads, the beach, in the mountains, in the snow that I decided to create a folder called "Moving Forward" and put these pictures in one place where I can easily find them. I encourage you to create your own "Moving Forward" folder of photos. You can continue to add to that folder through your journaling time and review the photos periodically to give you hope and encouragement on your trust journey.

Scripture

Read the following scriptures, and then on the journaling lines write down words that stand out to you from each of the verses.

I waited patiently for the LORD; he turned to me and heard my cry. He lifted me out of the slimy pit, out of the mud and mire; he set my feet on a rock and gave me a firm place to stand. He put a new song in my mouth, a hymn of praise to our God. Many will see and fear the LORD and put their trust in him.

PSALM 40:1-3

"I will lead the blind by ways they have not known, along unfamiliar paths I will guide them; I will turn the darkness into light before them and make the rough places smooth. These are the things I will do; I will not forsake them."

ISAIAH 42:16

"Remain in me, as I also remain in you. No branch can bear fruit by itself; it must remain in the vine. Neither can you bear fruit unless you remain in me."

JOHN 15:4

Playlist

"I'll Give Thanks," Housefires, featuring Kirby Kaple

"Peace Be Still," Hope Darst

"'Tis So Sweet to Trust in Jesus," Casting Crowns

Prayer

Along with using this guided prayer, write your own prayer.

Heavenly Father, I give You my anxieties, fears, and doubts related to trust. I don't have to feel ashamed that I have trust issues. I don't have to move forward more quickly than I'm ready. But at the same time, I'm not going to make excuses for not healing. I'm taking one step at a time, moving forward with You on this journey of growing in trust. Give me the courage, wisdom, and hope I need. Amen.

_____

_____

_____

_____

_____

_____

_____

_____

"*Remain in Me, and I in you. Just as the branch cannot bear fruit of itself but must remain in the vine, so neither can you unless you remain in Me.*"

JOHN 15:4 NASB

Chapter 1

Quietly Quitting on Hope

Moving forward in trusting others, God, and yourself is brave. It's the opposite of staying stuck, giving up, and quitting on hope.

This isn't to say you should feel bad for the moments you've done that or that you won't suddenly hit a place where you feel stuck again. That's normal. In fact, you might feel some resistance while you journal. That, too, is normal. You can pause if you need to, but don't let it stop you altogether. Keep moving forward in your healing journey.

I'm not sure which season you're in as you journal, but I'm in the Christmas season as I write.

One of my favorite things is to sit in a room lit only by the twinkly lights of my Christmas tree. I mean, really, can we just leave the tree up all year?

In this room filled with the glow of twinkly lights, I open my Christmas devotional where I read the familiar verses of Luke 1. These verses, however, were never meant to be just for Christmas. They are promises of hope all year long.

These are words from the familiar passage in Luke:

But Mary said to the angel, "How will this be, since I am a virgin?" The angel answered and said to her, "The Holy Spirit will come upon you, and the power of the Most High will overshadow you; for that reason also the holy Child will be called the Son of God. And behold, even your relative Elizabeth herself has conceived a son in her old age, and she who was called infertile is now in her sixth month. For nothing will be impossible with God." And Mary said, "Behold, the Lord's bond-servant; may it be done to me according to your word." And the angel departed from her. (Luke 1:34–38 NASB)

In these words I found a beautiful treasure for us: "For nothing will be impossible with God."

In all this moving forward on a new path of trust, it's not all up to us. We walk with God where nothing is impossible. Circumstances may not work out like we hope and pray, but that isn't an indication that the outcome was impossible for God. It means He's making another plan possible because He sees and knows things we don't. And from His unchanging goodness, He is leading elsewhere.

I don't know what you've been through and how deeply you've been hurt, but I do know that, just because your trust has been broken, it doesn't mean your joy has been stolen. My hope is that by the end of this journal you will be filled with more hope, joy, contentment, and peace than you could imagine.

Just as there will be glimmers of hope, there will be glimmers of joy and gladness as you move forward. Some will be because of sweet assurances and revelations from the Lord. Other glimmers of joy will be because, as you come out from the fog of pain, you'll start to notice simple joys again. He is providing those for you through a child's laughter, a sunrise with exquisite colors, twinkly lights on a tree, an unexpected blessing that comes your way, or a sweet note from a friend.

Remember, you didn't choose what happened when others broke your trust. But you do get to choose how you look at your life today. You get to choose to intentionally put things in your life that remind you of the goodness of God, and things that remind you to look for glimmers of joy and gladness. You don't have to quit on hope; you get to believe that with God, all things are possible.

For me, I just might leave my Christmas tree up longer this year. I mean, since it's not a real tree, I could keep redecorating it for every holiday that comes after Christmas. Too much? Maybe so. But I love that I get to choose that if I want to!

Guided Journaling

1. In this journal, we are going to do quite a bit of exploration. But here's what I want us to declare right from the beginning:

   I'm giving myself permission to do compassionate investigation and exploration. I don't want to use this journal as a place to further compound the hurt in me, nor do I want to compound bitterness because of the hurt done to me. I want to use this journal as a safe place to be honest with myself and with God for the purpose of learning, growing, changing what I can, and accepting the realities that are beyond my ability to change. There's been enough turmoil. Now I'm on a journey toward the peace Jesus promised could be mine even when the world around me isn't always peaceful.

   Write your own declaration about compassionate investigation and exploration here. Feel free to use some of the words I've used and add your own.

   _____

   _____

   _____

   _____

   _____

   _____

You didn't choose what happened when others broke your trust. But you do get to choose how you look at your life today.

Compassionate exploration doesn't mean stuffing hard feelings around deep woundings. We must be honest. The Psalms are full of very honest feelings and expressions and questions about pain and suffering. But even while we need to go there with the hard stuff, we don't want to park in the pit of it all. Think about the phrase "compassionate investigation and exploration" and how it relates to yourself, others, and God. Write your thoughts.

2. *Merriam-Webster*'s definition of *hope* is "to cherish a desire with anticipation: to want something to happen or be true."[1] When I think of this definition, I think of . . .

_____

_____

_____

_____

_____

_____

_____

_____

_____

_____

_____

_____

_____

3. What are your thoughts about the chapter title, "Quietly Quitting on Hope"? Where do you think this has played out in your life?

_____

_____

_____

_____

_____

_____

_____

_____

_____

_____

4. Can you name your specific disappointments when it comes to hope? Use the prompt "I really believed . . . ." For example, "I really believed this time my friend would be there for me." Or "I really believed this relationship would work out."

_____

_____

_____

_____

_____

_____

_____

_____

_____

_____

_____

_____

_____

5. How did those disappointments affect you? What story did you start to tell yourself as a result?

For me, I really believed my friends would all stick with me through the divorce. Many did, but others did not. The story I started telling myself was that people only want to be my friend as long as things are happy and easy. But when things get hard, people don't want to stick around. Therefore, it's better to fake being better than I am, or else I will risk losing all my friendships.

Journal your thoughts about the stories you've been telling yourself about disappointments.

It took me a while to realize it's not my responsibility to manage other people's feelings around my situation. I don't want to be a Debbie Downer, always complaining about my hardships, but I also don't want to pretend I'm fine when I'm not. I had to find the balance of sometimes processing the hard stuff and sometimes just getting together with friends to have a fun dinner and talk about other things.

The friends who were the most helpful for me were those who had also walked through brokenness in their lives and were committed to healing and moving forward in healthy ways. I learned to stop telling myself the story that all friends will eventually walk away from me in hard seasons. And this helped me drop some of my walls and guardedness so I could vulnerably connect with safe friends again. What are new, truthful stories you can tell yourself about these disappointments?

_____

_____

_____

_____

_____

6. For me, hope is either the most beautiful feeling of possibility or the worst feeling of defeat. To dare to hope is to simultaneously open up our greatest desires and our greatest fears.

   Reflecting on this, what is a small step you can take into possibilities instead of staying stuck in defeat or failure?

   _____

   _____

   _____

   _____

   _____

7. "But if we're not willing to risk hoping, then we are already quietly quitting on a better future. The hardships of today will feel so much heavier when we limit our view of life to the hardships of right now. We will trade dreaming for dread. We will exchange looking forward with joy for looking backward with sorrow. We will swap the anticipation of future possibilities for the angst of staying stuck in the pain of what happened."

   How do you relate to this quote from the book?

   _____

   _____

   _____

   _____

   _____

   _____

   _____

   _____

Action Steps

When we begin to heal from the hurt of broken trust, we'll feel all kinds of things—mad, bitter, sad, hopeless. Sometimes our feelings are directed at the person who betrayed us. (We'll do some exercises about that later.) However, we can also be hard on ourselves.

We fill ourselves with the weight of regret with statements like:

> *Why did I . . .*
> *Why didn't I . . .*
> *I should have . . .*
> *I shouldn't have . . .*
> *I can't believe I . . .*

An effective tool for healing from broken trust is to write a letter to yourself. You can write in your journal or on a separate sheet of paper.

You might want to use the prompts to express some of that regret. Then move into writing to yourself with compassion. If that's hard to do, imagine you're writing to a friend. What would you say to her? Sometimes we are so much kinder to others than we are to ourselves. But remember, this needs to be a letter to *you*.

In addition, these questions and statements might help you write the letter to yourself.

- What are you afraid of when it comes to hope and trust?
- "When you know better, you do better." How does this statement help you move forward?
- "I did the best I could at the time." Is this a helpful statement for letting go of regrets?
- How can you avoid victim mentality?
- How can you make sure not to shame yourself?
- Who can you trust and share with in your healing journey?
- Finish the thought: By the end of my processing through *The Trust Journey*, I want to be . . .

Write your letter here.

Scripture

Trust in him at all times, you people; pour out your hearts to him, for God is our refuge.

PSALM 62:8

He *will* lead you *in the way that you should go.* When you feel dried up *and worthless*, God will nourish you and give you strength. And you will grow like a garden *lovingly* tended; you will be like a spring whose water never runs out.

ISAIAH 58:11 VOICE

May the God of hope fill you with all joy and peace as you trust in him, so that you may overflow with hope by the power of the Holy Spirit.

ROMANS 15:13

Playlist

"Christ the Sure and Steady Anchor," Matt Boswell and Matt Papa

"God Is in This Story," Katy Nichole and Big Daddy Weave

"If I Could Have Anything," Housefires, featuring Blake Wiggins and Ahjah Walls

Prayer

Heavenly Father, as I journal, You know where I am with my feelings and thoughts about hope. You know where I've quit, where I've gotten stuck sometimes on anger or bitterness about the way things are. Forgive me for that and help me to entrust those things to You. Even with disappointments and discouragements, help me not to quit on hope. I'm looking forward to seeing how Your tender love helps me to heal and to grow. I want to keep moving forward with You. Amen.

Hope is either the most beautiful feeling of possibility or the worst feeling of defeat. To dare to hope is to simultaneously open up our greatest desires and our greatest fears.

Chapter 2

What Is This Feeling: Discernment or a Trigger?

A **text from someone I hadn't been in contact with for a long time** caught me off guard. Although I no longer thought too often about the hurt she'd caused me, this text led me to rehash our last encounter many years before. It had been such an emotional and damaging conversation. As I remembered it now, the shock of her breach of trust made my heart beat faster. The anxiety was intense, and I could feel the tears coming. There had been a few half-hearted attempts to heal our relationship. But it had been a huge betrayal, one I never could have imagined. I had decided the safest place for me was to have zero contact.

But now I sat with the text, remembering how close we'd been and wishing that hard thing hadn't come between us.

Her out-of-the-blue text came with apologies. I was immediately suspicious. What made her reach out now after so long? What was her motive? What did she want from me? I turned these thoughts over and over. What if I opened the door and responded, and instead of apologies the conversation became angry and she lashed out? She could be so unpredictable. On the other hand, what if something was going on with her that was really big? Would I regret not having contact? And what if we could actually have a friendship again?

And beyond all my fears, what did God want me to do? I'd processed all this with Him, I was sure I'd forgiven her, and I knew that forgiveness didn't always mean reconciliation. Maybe now was a time when I should reconsider.

Was I overreacting? Was the swirl of emotions I felt from this text just a trigger from the past, or was it discernment warning me this still wasn't a safe relationship?

I didn't know what to do. I got so stuck on the "what is the right thing to do?" question that I almost made myself sick. But then I realized the decision was just that—a decision that I would pray about and then was mine to make. There wasn't necessarily a right or wrong answer here. So I decided that writing down each choice I could possibly make in response would help me get unstuck. And then I would also respond to these questions: What thoughts does that decision lead me to have? How does that decision make me feel?

- I could do nothing. That's what I'd been choosing to do for years, and it was a decision that I could live with, even though it still sometimes made me sad.
- I could respond with a text asking for more information. "Thank you for your apology. It's been a long time, so I was surprised to see your text. What made you decide to reach out now?" This made me think, *We'll see.* I wouldn't know what I thought or felt until I got a response. Mostly I felt guarded.
- I could say, "Thank you for the apology. Do you want to have a phone conversation?" This choice made my heart pound and made me recoil as I remembered how she'd hurled so many hurts my way. I decided I was not in a place to have a phone conversation. That felt too scary and unpredictable. I didn't want to undo the peace and stability I'd worked hard to establish.

So I chose to text, "Thank you for your apology. It's been a long time, so I was surprised to see your text. What made you decide to reach out now?"

The reply I received helped clear up whether my hesitancy in responding was a trigger from what happened in the past or present-day discernment. She immediately texted: "Why do you care about my timing? Why can't you just accept my apology?"

I had my answer. That was not the reply I'd hoped for, but it revealed what I needed to know. It confirmed that I was discerning to be cautious for good reason.

I am wiser now. And based on a few other unsolicited follow-up texts from her, it was clear it was not wise to continue to open that door. It was not a safe place to reengage. I knew that exploring more with her would damage my heart and potentially derail me emotionally. My reengagement would not help the relationship to suddenly be healthy and could potentially pull me into having reactions that didn't reflect the health I'd worked so hard to pursue.

This boundary of not engaging in texts that are hostile, based on past experiences with her, was one I needed. This boundary was one I could live with. This boundary was one that helped me have healthier relationships now.

Wouldn't it be so much easier if relationships came with "How do I do this?" directions? That would make messy relationships so much easier to figure out. While we don't have clear-cut directions in relationships, we do have tools that we gain through reflection, prayer, and experiential wisdom. In this chapter about triggers and discernment, I hope your journaling will equip you with more tools and awareness you can use to make decisions about relationships like this.

Guided Journaling

1. In this chapter of the book I described a situation where I got triggered and all the confusion and fear that welled up inside of me. It was as if I couldn't tell the difference between then and now. It didn't matter that this was a completely different person; the feelings were the same. It felt as if the past was repeating itself. When you get triggered or have an out-of-proportion reaction to a situation that

tapped into some past hurt you've experienced, what happens to you emotionally and physically?

_____

_____

_____

_____

_____

_____

_____

_____

2. There seems to be a paper-thin line between healthy discernment and triggers caused by pain from the past.

My discernment rarely comes with immediate details. It's a feeling prompted by the Holy Spirit. My triggers rarely come with immediate details. They are feelings prompted by pain from my past.

I have to pray through and sort through both. And sometimes a trigger from a past situation provides experiential wisdom that ushers in discernment. Like I said, a paper-thin line.

Have you found it to be true that there's a paper-thin line between discernment and triggers? At this point have you determined a way to distinguish between the two? Write about that or what still confuses you.

_____

_____

_____

_____

The other day I got triggered over something and felt completely gripped by fear. I realized that whether I'm having discernment or I'm experiencing a trigger, I have to work really hard to not get consumed by a spirit of fear. I love being reminded of 2 Timothy 1:7 (ESV): "For God gave us a spirit not of fear but of power and love and self-control." When you read the words *power*, *love*, and *self-control*, what do they mean to you personally? And how can remembering this verse help you?

---

3. When I'm struggling with the fears of trusting someone that could potentially betray me, it's easy for me to jump to worst-case scenarios—because I've experienced worst-case scenarios. So when I asked my wise friend how to deal with this, without hesitation she replied, "Investigate." She didn't mean for me to get obsessive or to unnecessarily shop for pain. But if something doesn't add up, look into it further.

    What's your response to the advice to investigate? Have you done this previously in a situation where you were feeling unsure and unsafe? How did it go?

Friend, please lean in close here. It is okay for us to need more information. It is okay for us to ask questions and verify what is true. It is okay for us to be honest about what we can and cannot handle.

Let's further explore the idea of investigating. For some people and in some situations "investigate" might feel too strong for the situation. Maybe a better phrase is "get curious." Getting curious means exploring without being accusatory, without assuming the worst, without attaching my judgment to a situation before I know the facts. It means saying, *I wonder why I'm feeling this way.* Keep in mind your goal: you want to get to a place where you *respond* instead of *react.* Here are some ideas for ways to approach a situation with curiosity.

First, check yourself. Can you make sure you're calm before talking? Watch your body language. Are you coming across as hostile? An overly aggressive stance doesn't prompt honesty from the other person. Instead, it invites defensiveness and possibly secrecy.

In your conversation, share how you're feeling, what you're thinking, and how you're reacting. Then ask for more information. You can start the conversation with one of these prompts:

- Help me understand what just happened.
- I'm upset about what happened and want to get to a better place. Is this a good time to talk?
- Our relationship is important to me, and I want us to work this out. Can we talk?
- Can we pause for a minute? I need to understand this better.

Which of the above suggestions about getting curious can help you when you're ready to have needed conversations?

_____

_____

_____

_____

_____

_____

_____

_____

_____

_____

4. My counselor, Jim Cress, taught me that the human brain is always in search of confidence in knowing. In other words, as much as is possible, I have to know what's going on so I can be confident that I'm safe. But facts aren't the only things we need to pay attention to when assessing whether or not it is safe to trust another person. Feelings are also crucial. Safety is both fact and feeling.

How do you see facts and feelings playing out when it comes to trusting people? Write about what actions and feelings you need to see in a person for you to feel that it is a safe relationship and you can trust them.

_____

_____

_____

_____

_____

_____

_____

_____

_____

_____

5. When we dismiss our feelings and what those feelings are trying to tell us, our initial instinct can be to numb, ignore, override, or shame ourselves for having them. Do you dismiss your feelings by turning to one of these coping mechanisms? Or maybe something else?

_____

_____

_____

_____

_____

_____

_____

_____

_____

Some coping mechanisms can be useful for a time. For example, numbing can be a coping mechanism to protect ourselves from something that might be too overwhelming to process. The key is to make sure we don't impede our forward growth. We need to step from our coping mechanism to a way of processing that will lead us to healing. Write your thoughts about where you are in that process.

_____

_____

_____

_____

_____

_____

_____

_____

_____

_____

_____

6. Let's get back to dealing with our original question from the chapter title, "What Is This Feeling: Discernment or a Trigger?" In other words, is this warning feeling my discernment firing that something is wrong right now or a trigger from the past? I would propose to you, it's both. A trigger may mean that more healing is needed. Discernment may be telling us to take it slow. Our past informs us about what can go wrong. Our present discernment reminds us to investigate. If both are done with the motivation of our need for safety, then there should be lots of grace for this desire, especially when we've been repeatedly hurt.

Ongoing healing, allowing time to pass, taking into account our pasts, asking questions to investigate, and extending ourselves grace: How have these been helpful in your healing process?

7. When trust has been broken in a relationship, trust issues can only be worked on in the context of relationship. That doesn't mean we need to return to that previous relationship where we got hurt in order to work on trust. If that's possible, then great. But sometimes that may not be possible or safe. What it does mean is that we can't isolate ourselves and work on repairing trust alone. If trust was broken because of a relationship, trust has to be repaired through safe connection in another relationship.

How do you feel about working out trust issues in the context of a relationship? If you've already experienced some healing through a trustworthy relationship, write about that. If you find yourself hesitant to move forward in trusting someone, explore that in your journaling. What are some of your fears about trusting? About letting go of distrust?

8. I touched on the suitcase situation in the book's chapter and share that a similar situation eventually happened with a safe man who was willing to lean in when I pulled back. A man who was willing to unpack what I was feeling without personalizing it and getting defensive, make a plan for the future, and give me access to any other information about his activities and whereabouts. Because of the way he responded, I really didn't need any more information. What I needed more than anything to feel safe and to feel like he was trustworthy was a response that communicated that he cared about what I cared about. If it was a concern to me, it was something for us to talk about.

I hope you've had responses like this that have made you feel safe, heard, and validated. Can you take a moment to write about a response you've had in a relationship that made you feel that way—and one that did not?

9. One of the most important truths I've realized is this: This new person in my life didn't fix my trust issues. That was an inside job I had to work on for several years before I ever met him. What are some insights you've had about the internal work you need to do?

Friend, please lean in close here. It is okay for us to need more information. It is okay for us to ask questions and verify what is true. It is okay for us to be honest about what we can and cannot handle.

Action Steps

Trusted friends bring a sense of security and safety. And as we've discussed in this chapter, at least some of our healing must be worked out in safe relationships. If you have a trusted friend, write a prayer of thanks. And maybe even send them a thank-you text or note. If your trusted person is someone you live with, reach out to them with a sincere thank-you and hug.

If you don't have a trustworthy person in your life, I encourage you to start praying for God to send you that person. Maybe it's someone you already know, and you can now choose to take your friendship to a deeper level. Write a prayer below asking God for a support system of trusted friends. What is one action step you can take? Write that down and give yourself a deadline to hold yourself accountable.

Scripture

I will always look to you, as you stand beside me and protect me from fear. With all my heart, I will celebrate, and I can safely rest. I am your chosen one. You won't leave me in the grave or let my body decay. You have shown me the path to life, and you make me glad by being near to me. Sitting at your right side, I will always be joyful.

PSALM 16:8–11 CEV

But test everything that is said. Hold on to what is good. Stay away from every kind of evil. Now may the God of peace make you holy in every way, and may your whole spirit and soul and body be kept blameless until our Lord Jesus Christ comes again. God will make this happen, for he who calls you is faithful.

1 THESSALONIANS 5:21–24 NLT

God has not given us a spirit of timidity, but of power and love and discipline.

2 TIMOTHY 1:7 NASB

Playlist

"He Sees You," Terrian

"Way Maker," Caleb & Kelsey

"You Will Be Found," Natalie Grant and Cory Asbury

Prayer

Heavenly Father, You know the hurts in me, the situations that trigger me and cause me to doubt that I can trust others, myself, and sometimes You. I'm learning so much about how I'm wired, what triggers me and causes me to respond in unhelpful ways. Help me move forward in ways that will help me have the trusting relationships I so desire. I want to be able to trust others, but I'm afraid I'll experience more hurt. Show me how to trust the discernment You give me that will allow me to connect with safe and trustworthy people. Amen.

Chapter 3

Red Flags and the Roots of Distrust

y friend Mel was traveling with me on my way to a speaking engagement. The hotel where we were staying had very complicated parking, so we used the valet service. As we got ready to leave the hotel for the church, Mel went to the valet desk to request our vehicle while I stayed in the room to finish getting ready.

By the time I got downstairs, Mel had our rental car ready, so I hopped in the car and got all situated. While I was fiddling with the air-conditioning vents, Mel said she was having a hard time getting the car into drive. So I glanced over to the console where the gearshift was located. As I did, I noticed a golf ball that hadn't been there the day before.

"Mel, where did this golf ball come from?"

At that moment Mel got a very concerned look on her face. "Lysa, this isn't our car!"

What?!

I jumped out of the car while loudly declaring, "Oh no, this isn't our car! *That's* our car," and I pointed to the car behind us.

The people on the sidewalk witnessing this whole ordeal started dying laughing. One woman asked, "How in the world did you make that mistake? The two cars don't look even remotely alike!"

And she was right.

While I put my stuff into the correct car, Mel talked to the valet guys. Then I noticed the owner of the vehicle we had almost stolen walking up to his car and checking the three golf bags in the back. Obviously he and a couple of friends had traveled to play at a course nearby.

He was about to get into his car when Mel ran back to the car, opened the driver's side back door, and said, "Sorry, sir, I just have to get all my stuff out of your car." He was so confused. He had absolutely no idea how close we had come to stealing his vehicle.

Can you imagine if we had ignored the golf ball and the different gearshift? We would have driven off in the wrong car with not a care in the world. We would have gone to the church—in an essentially *stolen* vehicle—where I would have preached my little heart out.

Meanwhile, that man would have spent his entire day not on the golf course but filing police reports, checking the hotel security cameras, and making sure someone was about to get charged with grand theft auto. And that somebody would have been me!

This story still makes me laugh, so I couldn't resist sharing it.

Sometimes life can get moving so fast we stop paying attention to the details. Specifically in relationships, the details I'm talking about are red flags. Every relationship will have its challenges that need to be talked through and worked on. But in some situations, those challenges are more like warnings. And so I call them red flags—reasons to pause, consider what is really going on, seek out wisdom, be honest about what you are seeing, play out how this could affect the future, and pray through what needs to be done.

Sometimes busyness and getting through hectic seasons are the reasons we don't see or address the red flags in a relationship. But other times it's because either we don't want to see them or we don't know what to do, so we just hope the concerns get better over time. I've ignored red flags for all these reasons. And I wish I hadn't.

My counselor, Jim, has reminded me often that when you know better, you do better.

I'm really trying to do better at recognizing red flags and not jumping to the extremes of overreacting or underreacting.

Let's dive into this a little more in our journaling time.

Guided Journaling

1. Red flags aren't there to annoy you or be a killjoy; they're there to protect you. In the same way, red flags in our relationships alert us to issues we need to pay closer attention to and probably address. Red flags we ignore don't typically fix themselves—they just become more and more of an issue. Eventually, they can grow into serious breaches of trust. So it's important to be aware of these red flags, these warnings that something is off with someone we are in a relationship with.

   Think about a time when you ignored a red flag and it ended up damaging your trust in that relationship. Instead of dealing with it, what did you do? What do you wish you had done? (Remember, we are showing ourselves compassion. We're looking at the past to learn from it, not to be filled with regrets.)

2. When it comes to red flags, most of the time I will start to have a gut feeling of discernment that keeps pricking at my thoughts and won't go away. I've always described discernment as a deep-down knowing. It's the ability to pick up cues that allow us to recognize subtle differences and inconsistencies, perceive when something isn't as it should be, and instinctively feel when someone is being dishonest. What are your thoughts about your discernment? What role has it played—or not played—in a relationship where trusting that person is sometimes an issue?

3. Trust requires the feeling of safety and connection in a relationship. In this chapter I wrote, "Hyper desires for safety can mean low levels of connection. Hyper desires for connection can mean low levels of safety."

   Explore these statements, writing down what you've noticed about yourself being "hyper" or extreme when it comes to either connection or safety. For me, I've struggled with wanting safety so much that I sometimes avoid taking the risks required for connection. Write about your desires and/or struggles with trust when you think of the words *safety* and *connection*.

4. Some people believe that when you love someone, you must give them unconditional trust. I understand the sentiment of this. I wish there was absolutely no chance for either person to make decisions that break trust. But we all know that's not possible on this side of eternity. So instead of shooting for unconditional trust where we are blind to red flags and are expected to overlook them, we need to shift to wise trust. What are your thoughts about blind trust versus wise trust?

When considering the difference, I think of this saying: When people show you who they are, believe them.[2] I think some people tend to be very trusting, and their hearts are filled with so much compassion that this can lead them to ignore red flags; in other words, they ignore what people's actions are showing them. On the other hand, some people fall on the other end of the spectrum in that they don't trust anyone. Their paranoia and suspicions cause them to assign untrustworthy motives to actions that might be innocent and situations that might be safe. Do you tend to be more trusting or skeptical? How does that play out for you? Do you think you need to make any adjustments in this when moving forward in safe relationships?

5. In the book I included a list of eleven red flags that can be a tool to help you pinpoint your concerns about trust. Red flags in our relationships alert us to issues we need to pay closer attention to and probably address. I explain that this isn't something we want to use against another person in accusatory ways or to unnecessarily stir up issues. But it is a tool to help us find some much-needed clarity, discernment, and possibly the language to have healthy, productive conversations. We can use this list to better understand the red flags we are sensing, and where the roots of our distrust may be coming from.

This list of red flags is a lot to process, so I want you to take time to unpack these. You might want to return to this list many times to process various situations and relationships. For now, let's review the eleven red flags. After each, write a brief summary of what each red flag means to you.

- Incongruity _____

- Inconsistency _____

- Insincerity _____

- Self-centeredness _____

- Insecurity _____

- Immaturity _____

- Immorality _____

- Insubordination _____

- Incompetence _____

- Irresponsibility _____

- Inflated sense of self _____

6. It's one thing to identify red flags, but it's equally crucial to assess how serious the red flags are that we are discerning. Some guidelines I gave you for determining the seriousness of a red flag are five spectrums:

   - Spectrum of severity: Is this critical or minor?
   - Spectrum of occurrence: Is this a pattern or occasional?
   - Spectrum of risk: How much will this potentially cost you emotionally, financially, mentally, spiritually, or physically?
   - Spectrum of proximity: How often do you interact with this person?
   - Spectrum of tolerance: In this season of your life, how much of this are you willing to tolerate?

   Let's apply what we've learned. In the list in the previous question, put a check by the red flags that are concerning but not super serious to you right now, perhaps using the five spectrums to help you determine that. Now put a star by the one(s) that is most serious to you right now, and again use the five different spectrums to help you determine that. You might want to write a person's name by the red flag.

7. As you're learning about red flags, you might realize your heart is making excuses or covering up for someone while trying to quiet the warnings your brain is sending you. What are you saying outwardly that doesn't match what you are feeling inwardly? These could be indications that you're ignoring red flags.

_____

_____

_____

_____

_____

Let's pause on that. We choose not to deal with red flags for so many reasons. One of my friends said she didn't address the red flags in her marriage because she was fearful of a worst-case scenario. What if bringing up issues just compounded the difficulties in the marriage? What if her husband wanted a divorce? When she thought about the impact of separation or divorce, especially to her kids, she knew she wasn't ready to have conversations that might require final decisions.

A few years down the road, however, she was ready. She had gotten to a place where she was paying too great a price for not addressing the red flags. Although her hope was that they could repair the relationship, she knew that if the marriage ended, she could handle it. She had many difficult conversations with her husband. And her husband agreed to get counseling. After a couple years of really working on their marriage, they had a stronger marriage than before.

A couple of things to note here. On one hand, it can be helpful to think of the worst-case possibilities so you can begin to process if you can live with that outcome. After all, we really don't know how a conversation will turn out. My friend's marriage could have ended in divorce. On the other hand, defaulting to extremes can be harmful. We can make inaccurate conclusions about what those difficult conversations will lead to.

The reality is that not every conversation is going to end in a worst-case scenario. There are many possible outcomes to difficult conversations. Many times the outcome is somewhere in the middle, where we address the issues and work on them. We can't let our fears of worst-case scenarios cause us to ignore red flags in our relationships. This eventually catches up with us and probably leads to even worse trust issues in our relationships.

Do you tend to ignore red flags or address them? Write about a time that ignoring red flags affected a relationship. Maybe you've addressed some red flags. Choose one situation and write about what you said and how the conversation went.

8. Red flags we ignore don't typically just go away. I've thought so much about why I ignored red flags in the past. I was definitely similar to my friend in that I wasn't ready to make any final decisions about my marriage.

But here's another reason. I liked conflict-free living. I wanted everyone to get along, for no feathers to be ruffled. And I wanted to avoid any conversations that I feared wouldn't go well. So you know what I did? I swept things under the rug. I told myself it wasn't that big of a deal. I was being dramatic. Why create a big situation? I tried harder and harder to please and to make things work. I hoped in time that things would just get better.

I've talked to so many women who, like me, kept quiet about concerns in a relationship. Many of us have been conditioned to be this way. To be nice, polite, and quiet. As a result, it can feel wrong and so uncomfortable to speak up. Whatever the reason, I hope that you will pray about using your voice and saying hard and truthful things if that's where God leads you. Remember we are un-learning some things that haven't fostered trusting relationships. And often some of the things we thought were biblical really are not.

I read a verse that sheds light on speaking up. Proverbs 3:3 says, "Do not let kindness and truth leave you" (NASB). Kindness and truth go hand in hand. In the past I thought kindness meant not saying hard things. And sometimes it does. But not always. Kindness can lead us to have truthful conversations because our ultimate goal is to have a better relationship founded on truth, authenticity, vulnerability, and trust.

If you've ignored red flags in the past, now might be the time to make a different decision—to address the red flags. Do you recognize in yourself any of the reasons I shared about why I ignored red flags? Or maybe other reasons come to mind. What are your thoughts about the verse about kindness and truth and how that could help you move forward?

9. When we're healing from trust issues and learning to have needed conversations, we don't have to start with the most difficult ones. I became aware that good relationships could be strengthened if I was willing to address trust concerns instead of letting them build up. Even in good relationships, red flags may pop up from time to time. Maybe your feelings of alarm need a clarifying conversation to determine this isn't a real red flag, just a misunderstanding. Or maybe the red flag is being caused by a small issue with a minor impact. Please know a red flag doesn't always mean the relationship is destined to fall apart. It may simply mean some work needs to be done and some intentional and honest conversations need to take place instead of letting these things fester in a relationship.

   Think about a good relationship where there's a small issue with minor impact, but it still bothers you and negatively affects what is an otherwise good relationship. Write down the conversation you'd like to have with this person. You can start with something like, "Can we talk about something that's been bothering me? We have such a good friendship, and I don't want anything to mess that up."

Now, is this a conversation you're ready to have? Only you can decide that. Only you can honor what's important to you and honor the relationship at the same time. Pray about it and commit to when you're going to have the conversation, and then have it! Come back here and record how it went.

_____

_____

_____

_____

_____

_____

_____

_____

_____

_____

_____

_____

_____

_____

_____

_____

_____

Trust requires the feeling of safety and connection in a relationship.

10. Now let's look at a conversation that's needed in a more serious red flag situation, maybe one you identified when journaling #5 and #6. These are the conversations where we think, *I want to trust you, but I don't.* Having this conversation might seem terrifying. Especially if you've let things go and ignored red flags. Especially if deep down you fear it's a conversation that could go in a direction that could irrevocably affect the relationship.

   For now, write down the name of the person and some details in the more serious red flag situation. Start praying about the needed conversation. *Lord, You know the red flags I need to address in this relationship. You know what I need to say and do. Give me wisdom for knowing if and when to have this conversation and courage to say what I need to say to move forward in trust. Amen.*

   Write any more thoughts or prayers about this situation.

_____

_____

_____

_____

_____

_____

_____

_____

_____

_____

We'll continue to explore these weightier conversations in the next chapter. I know there's a lot to think about, pray about, and process. Keep coming back to this chapter to review and apply its lessons to additional situations in your moving-forward journey. Keep in mind your goal: fostering trusting relationships. This is brave work, friend. I'm praying for you.

Action Steps

Sometimes we need to get out of our heads and let some other forms of creativity flow. Even if you don't consider yourself especially skilled at these, give one a try! You might want to play songs from the playlists found in each chapter of *The Trust Journey* while you create.

Think about various paths your feet have literally and figuratively walked on in moving forward. Where have your steps taken you, and where do you want them to take you when it comes to trust? Now try reflecting this in a painting, drawing, collage, 3D art, or some other form of creative artwork. Or maybe music is more your thing. Can you write or play a song that reflects your trust journey? And don't forget to keep adding photos to your Moving Forward folder. Maybe take a photo of what you created and add it to your folder.

Scripture

Trust in the LORD and do good; live in the land and cultivate faithfulness. Delight yourself in the LORD; and He will give you the desires of your heart. Commit your way to the LORD, trust also in Him, and He will do it. He will bring out your righteousness as the light, and your judgment as the noonday.

PSALM 37:3–6 NASB

"When He, the Spirit of truth, has come, He will guide you into all truth; for He will not speak on His own authority, but whatever He hears He will speak; and He will tell you things to come."

JOHN 16:13 NKJV

I pray that your love will overflow more and more, and that you will keep on growing in knowledge and understanding.

PHILIPPIANS 1:9 NLT

Playlist

"Breathe," Maverick City Music, featuring Chandler Moore, Jonathan McReynolds, and DOE

"The Lord Will Provide," Passion and Landon Wolfe

"Open the Eyes of My Heart," Michael W. Smith

Prayer

Lord, You know places where I've missed red flags of untrustworthy people, or places where I had hints of the red flags but I chose to ignore them and got hurt as a result. Help me be wise and brave as I move forward, and help me see what I need to see, know what I need to know, and do what I need to do to have trusting relationships. Let me approach relationships with wisdom, love, truth, and kindness. Thank You for the trustworthy relationships I have now, and show me ways to be a trustworthy person too. In Jesus' name, amen.

Chapter 4

Rips and Repairs

T he only experience I've ever had with sewing was when I felt compelled to sew during my pregnancy with my first daughter. I don't know why I thought it would be more motherly to sew my baby's crib bumper pads and coverlet, but that's what I told myself. Now, mind you, I didn't know how to sew, and at that time, there were no YouTube tutorials.

Despite it being a bit of a debacle, I did learn a little about sewing after getting a more experienced family member involved. When you first sew fabric together, you use large basting stitches. These are temporary stitches meant only to hold seams together until you sew the smaller, more permanent stitches. Seams held together with the larger stitches can easily be ripped apart. But pulling apart the seams with the smaller, more permanent stitches isn't so easy.

As I think about my sewing adventure, I remember a phrase about relationships: "the ties that bind." What a beautiful picture of an intimate relationship. The invisible emotional threads of connection stitch a love story held together by the threads of honesty, vulnerability, faithfulness, and trustworthiness.

The more the two people honor these threads of connection, the stronger the relationship becomes. The stronger the connection, the more assured both people are in the quality of the trusting relationship. But as time goes by, struggles pull at the relationship. Small rips go untended. Sharp words. Misunderstandings. Cold hearts. Seams loosen and pull apart.

One day you notice the fabric needs repair, so you take a closer look to see how you can mend it. You pull at this thread, asking questions about things that have bothered you. Another pull on a loose thread leads you to investigate red flags you've previously overlooked. The relationship, and maybe you, experience some unraveling. While you can't see clearly how to put things back the same way, you realize that maybe the unraveling was needed because you didn't know how loose the seams had become.

With time, patience, praying, talking, and trustworthy actions, the relationship can be repaired. It probably won't look the same. But this time the ties that bind might be even stronger.

Before we get into the guided journaling, let's do a practical exercise that might prove to be very helpful in a relationship where the threads are being loosened by everyday rips that need to be tended to. For me, the hardest part of starting this process of repair is to know how to communicate what's wrong.

I've learned it's helpful for me to have a framework to follow when starting conversations about everyday issues that are creating wear and tear on the relationship. For example, it's not a complete rupture of trust when someone shows up late to plans I've made with them. But when it is a consistent pattern, I feel like I can't count on that person and like I'm not a priority to them.

In a situation like this, over time, little rips get bigger and bigger. So the earlier we address the situation, the better. Here's a framework I came up with that really helps me. In a non-accusatory way, I communicate these things with this person.

5-Step Framework for a Repair Conversation

1. **Feeling:** This is what I'm feeling.
2. **Feeding this feeling:** This is what is feeding this feeling.
3. **Facts of this situation:** These are the facts. (Both you and the other person can share your facts here.)
4. **Figure out:** Figure out and process what I need or desire. (You may want to also

listen to what the other person needs to set them up for success so each of you understands the other's needs and desires.)

5. **Forward**: And finally, let's make a plan to move forward in a better way since we've had this conversation.

We will journal through a conversation you need to have using this framework. But I also want to acknowledge that while many of our relationships would benefit greatly from conversations like this, there may be a relationship in your life where the seams have been ripped and ruptured beyond this kind of mending.

How shocking it is to pull a thread and see the seams come apart—completely. When you make discoveries of patterns that are deeply concerning to you, and there's a refusal on their part to acknowledge the damage being done, the unraveling can terrify you and make you feel helpless. You exhaust yourself trying to fix what just continues to fall apart, and then right before your eyes it completely comes apart.

And the final heartbreaking discovery: the ties that bind us are incredibly strong until they become fragile because of the choices that are made. While this feels devastating— and it is—you'll discover that even though the relationship is irreparable, *you* are not irreparable. This is where you have an important decision to make: What do you do with your ripped-apart life? Who do you trust with your ripped-apart heart?

Although you're angry and shocked and justified in your harsh feelings, how are these feelings going to serve you? You'll see that staying in this place where you hold tightly to outrage, bitterness, or unforgiveness only robs you of peace and joy. By no means am I telling you not to deal with the situation or sweep the pieces of your broken heart under the rug. Not at all. This journal is all about dealing with reality, including emotions. At the same time, you have a brave decision to make: Will you choose to trust God with the remnants of your broken heart?

I realize this decision takes prayer and time. I know . . . I've been right in that place where I had the same choice you have. Over time I chose to trust God. God has given us a promise for when we feel like we're falling apart: "He is before all things, and in him all things hold together" (Colossians 1:17).

God holds you and your broken heart together. So gather up the remnants of your brokenness. Unclench the tight grip you have on fear and hurt and unforgiveness and release them to His hands. He's ready to walk with you as you trust Him.

Guided Journaling

1. As we journal through this chapter, we'll look at repairing rips in relationships. My counselor says, "For every rip, there needs to be a repair." When it comes to rips and repairs, we need to consider if we're dealing with a low-impact or high-impact broken trust situation. The high-level broken trust relationships are the ones that have the greatest intimacy but also the greatest risks and consequences. In the previous chapter, I walked you through having a conversation with someone in a low-impact broken trust relationship. Now let's look at high-impact broken trust.

    These are some of the key realizations I want you to walk away with after journaling in this chapter: The deeper the hurt, the longer the journey will be to recovery. No part of repairing severely broken trust should be done quickly. It takes time and believable behavior to establish a new track record. Don't rush past that. I want this to be one of the statements you forever carry with you. Trust takes time plus believable behavior, along with consistency, so a solid track record can be established.

    Time. Believable behavior. Consistency. Solid track record. That's the recipe for repairing rips in a high-impact broken trust situation. You might write that down in your journal or display it somewhere you can see it often. What are your thoughts about these necessary components for repairing trust?

_____

_____

_____

_____

_____

_____

_____

2. Now let's look at a relationship of high-impact broken trust that needs to be repaired. In the previous chapter you wrote down the name of a person who fits this category. Write the name of that person again here. Throughout this chapter, let's focus on that one relationship.

_____

The thing that makes high-impact broken trust take so long to repair is that you're not just having to address the hurtful behavior. The character and integrity issues inside the offender are the real driving force for why the behavior occurred in the first place. Their choices are an outward sign indicating inward problems that may require specialized therapy. As my counselor wisely taught me, "What people don't work out, they act out." Don't miss this reality.

In several of my relationships I discovered I was carrying the burden of figuring out how to fix everything. I wanted to fix what I might be doing wrong, I wanted to fix their issues, I wanted to fix the relationship, and I wanted to fix the consequences of this broken trust. Instead of letting the other people experience the consequences of their choices, I took on the burden of constantly providing safety nets so everything wouldn't fall apart. I just wanted it all to go away. I didn't want to enable the other people's poor choices. But I was also afraid that their consequences would make me suffer. And I was so terrified of the fallout.

What part of this do you relate to? Do you ever take on the burden of trying to fix this other person? What might you need to change so that you aren't working harder on them than they are working on themselves?

3. Let's unpack more about what the other person did to break trust with you. One way to do that is to ask yourself, *What is the root of my distrust here?* In parentheses after the list of possibilities below, you'll see the red flags from the last chapter listed again along with root causes, so you can continue making progress with what you've been learning. Consider: Is this breach of trust an issue because of their lack of . . .

- integrity? (immorality, incongruity)
- competence? (incompetence)
- reliability? (irresponsibility, inconsistency)
- care and compassion? (insincerity, self-centeredness)
- good judgment? (insubordination, immaturity)
- humility? (inflated sense of self)
- stability? (insecurity)

In many cases, it will be a combination of several of these. And often when these breaches of trust are combined with a lack of communication, it's like pouring gasoline on a fire—the damage is accelerated. Write down your insights about the root cause(s) of the rips in the relationship you've been journaling about.

---

4. When it comes to repairing a relationship, defining what you need to feel safe in this relationship will help you move forward.

My list is included here:

- To be who they say they are
- To do what they say they are going to do
- To show up with care and compassion
- To tell the truth
- To use good judgment and biblical wisdom with their decisions

I also talked to others about what they need from a trustworthy relationship. Note that this list includes behaviors we need to see in the other person—doing what they say they will do, for example. And it includes ways we need a person to interact with us, such as showing us patience with our doubts and fears.

Here's what others said:

- They are authentic.
- They never say, "I probably shouldn't share this, but . . ."
- They show consistency in how they treat you.
- They aren't moody, unpredictable, or prone to angry outbursts.
- They are resourceful.
- You can count on them to be there for you.
- They have longevity in their other relationships.
- They have a good reputation.
- They are loyal.
- They treat all people fairly.
- They are humble enough to admit they are sometimes wrong.
- They are willing to be held accountable.
- They don't dance around issues and are willing to be straightforward.
- They are available.
- They are cooperative.
- They don't cut corners or cheat.
- They respect other people's property.
- They respect your time.

That's a long list, isn't it? Yours can be too. This is a time to be honest with yourself and God. A gentle reminder: your needs matter. So make your list of what you need from the other person—qualities in them and ways they interact with you or respond to you—to establish a trustworthy relationship.

And to be clear, this list is not a list of demands we're going to hurl at this person. Many of the items on your list can be talked through one at a time. Some may not need to be talked about at all. As you navigate these conversations, the outcome will reveal what you need to know about repairing this relationship—or not. You may discover that some items on your list can be navigated together, while others are nonnegotiables. Write your list of qualities you need to have a trustworthy relationship.

5. The biggest factor for me to determine if I'm still safe with this person is how they react to my concerns. Remember the suitcase situation in chapter 2? This was a situation with a safe man, but it was triggering all kinds of reactions from my past. The difference? In this new relationship this man was willing to lean in, to hear how I felt, and to respond to what I needed. This was such a key part of feeling safe with him. I discovered that one of my nonnegotiables was a willingness to calmly process whatever my concerns were.

How other people respond to our need to explore issues of trust can reveal so much about their willingness to repair trust. What types of responses are green flags for you? What type of responses are red flags or nonnegotiables for you?

----

6. Now let's revisit the 5-Step Framework, listed below. This is one of the tools you can use for having a conversation with the person with whom you've experienced high-impact broken trust. You can think through these steps or write them out in preparation for the conversation.

5-Step Framework for a Repair Conversation
1. **Feeling:** This is what I'm feeling.
2. **Feeding this feeling:** This is what is feeding this feeling.
3. **Facts of this situation:** These are the facts. (Both you and the other person can share your facts here.)
4. **Figure out:** Figure out and process what I need or desire. (You may want to also listen to what the other person needs to set them up for success you both understand each other's needs and desires.)
5. **Forward:** And finally, let's make a plan to move forward in a better way since we've had this conversation.

Now, is it time to have the conversation with the person with whom you've experienced high-impact broken trust? The thought of having the needed conversation can seem daunting. You might want to default to simply putting it off, as you have before. Your anxiety may skyrocket. You may feel physically sick. Keep praying about it, and remember, you don't have to cover all your concerns at once. But you do need to start talking. Ignoring red flags does not make them go away. You've learned new tools to help you navigate this situation.

Some tips: Can you walk through the conversation with a counselor or trusted friend? Another way to practice the conversation is to use the "imaginary chair." Sit across from an empty chair. Imagine the person is sitting in the chair. Practice this talk and write out your conversation here. Now say what you need to say.

_____

_____

_____

_____

---

7. There are people who commit life-altering betrayals fraught with ongoing deception, lack of concern for the damage they've caused, and deep-seated character issues that will make trying to repair trust a futile pursuit. It's impossible to repair and build trust that keeps getting broken. If someone hasn't come completely clean about the extent of their betrayal with as full a disclosure as you want, then working on trusting them will just create more and more pain. I hope with all my heart that you never have this reality in your life. But if you do, at what point do you say enough is enough? Ask the Lord to reveal to you this week through prayer and reading Scripture, other messages you've heard, and conversations with trusted, wise advisors what you may need to consider at this point. When you are ready, journal your prayers and thoughts about this.

_____

_____

_____

_____

_____

8. When considering this decision, I had the weirdest sensation that this was the moment of transition between the life I'd fought so desperately to keep and the life I would step into where everything was different. I whispered the only prayer I could: "Jesus, I love You, and You love me. That's all I've got."

   Maybe you haven't had that transition yet, but you are becoming more and more certain that it's time to make that final decision to leave the past behind and to step forward. Or maybe you've already made that decision. It took many years for me to get to this point. For you, it may take a long time or not. Reflect on that and record anything you know you may need to declare to yourself at this point to help you not look back with regret. For example, I wrote a declaration to myself that I wouldn't look at this decision as something I made lightly. And that I wouldn't look back minimizing or doubting the severity of what I'd experienced.

_____

_____

_____

_____

_____

_____

_____

_____

9. Getting to that point was a journey of praying, trying, thinking, getting godly counsel, crying, trying again and again, time passing, and then knowing. Although I was devastated, I also was ready. And ready doesn't mean you have the future all figured out in a way you know will make you happier. It doesn't mean that you're not heartbroken and aren't gutted by deep grief.

No, it means that right now, because you have been seeking God and pleading for Him to repair the relationship or give you the strength to create boundaries, to make significant changes, or to step away, you know what to do. Are you at that point of knowing what to do? Write about it here. And if you're not at the point to make a final decision, that's okay too. Write about that.

_____

_____

_____

_____

_____

_____

_____

_____

_____

10. If this high-impact broken trust relationship is one of your most intimate relationships, the possible consequence of this conversation is significant. This is not a situation to navigate alone. Bring in your closest friends for support, biblical wisdom, and prayer. Tell them what's going on and that you really need them. I had times in the early, early morning and late, late nights that were especially difficult for me. I could call my friends who were also going through a similar thing, and I knew they would be there for me. In turn, I was there for them. They stayed at my house until

they were ready to be on their own. We had constant contact during the hardest times because the ending was really scary. It's okay if you feel that way too. Also, you've heard me mention my counselor, Jim Cress, previously. His wise input and therapeutic guidance during this most difficult time was invaluable.

What kind of support do you need from your friends and other trusted people who have your best interest in mind? Have you communicated this to them? Do you need to do that now?

_____

_____

_____

_____

_____

_____

_____

_____

11. Now have the conversation. Maybe it's a relationship of high-impact broken trust and you're at the point where you need to have honest and direct conversations to help improve and save the relationship. Or maybe you're at the point where you know that you are ready to say, "This has to change."

Some things to consider before the actual conversation:

- Pray for wisdom for the right time and the right way to have this conversation.
- It's better to avoid having these types of talks when anger or other intense feelings are present, so you might need to let some time pass. However, don't put it off out of fear.
- Do something to help you feel as calm and steady as you can before the conversation. Go for a walk, listen to worship music, or write out your thoughts before having the conversation.

- You might want a counselor or a trusted third party present.
- If you don't have someone present during the conversation, make sure a trusted person knows when you'll have this conversation.

Come back here and write about this conversation.

_____

_____

_____

_____

_____

_____

_____

_____

_____

_____

_____

_____

You've processed so much, friend. Every step of this trust journey is a way to honor yourself and, most importantly, God. When the consequences of this conversation feel hard and sad and heavy, remind yourself that you made decisions prayerfully, carefully, and wisely.

Action Steps

As I said at the beginning of this chapter, I am not a girl who sews. But I am a girl who looks to see visually what I'm experiencing internally. If you already have sewing supplies, stitch together something that will remind you of the threads of a trusting relationship with God or another person. If you don't have any materials with threads, consider purchasing a small kit, maybe for knitting, crocheting, needlepointing, or cross-stitching, and put that together. Or maybe make a friendship bracelet. You could do something as simple as this: put a trinket, like a heart, on a piece of yarn or ribbon and hang it where you'll see it daily.

Let the threads of this project remind you of the threads of God's love holding you together and the ties that bind you to another person in a safe relationship.

Time. Believable behavior. Consistency. Solid track record. That's the recipe for repairing rips in a high-impact broken trust situation.

Scripture

Taste of His goodness; see how wonderful the Eternal truly is. Anyone who puts trust in Him will be blessed *and comforted.*

PSALM 34:8 VOICE

There is a time for everything, and a season for every activity under the heavens . . . a time to tear and a time to mend, a time to be silent and a time to speak.

ECCLESIASTES 3:1, 7

He is before all things, and in him all things hold together.

COLOSSIANS 1:17

Playlist

"He Will Hold Me Fast," Selah

"Just Be Held," Casting Crowns

"You Hold It All Together," Maverick City Music, UPPERROOM, Chandler Moore and Elyssa Smith

Prayer

Heavenly Father, I'm learning some rips in relationships can be repaired. But some relationships are ruptured beyond repair, and I need to let go of them. I am seeking You to know what to do with each relationship. Give me courage and strength for both the letting go and the moving forward. The rips have caused me to be fearful about trusting anyone—sometimes even You, God. I release my tight grip on sadness, fear, hurt, bitterness, distrust, and unforgiveness. I'm trusting You. Tie my heart to Yours, God. Amen.

Chapter 5

And I Didn't Want to Be Alone

*A*lone **is missing a friendship you thought would last forever but** didn't. *Alone* means no longer having that one person to text or call every day. It's standing in Lowe's wishing you had that person to ask what you need so you can fix that thing you never thought you'd have to fix. *Alone* is two kids who are sick in the middle of the night and all you want is some sleep and someone else to help. It's missing family events because you can't be around that certain person until repairs have been made.

But when you think about adding the possible heartbreak that could happen when you try to move forward in a new relationship? Well, maybe *alone* doesn't seem all that bad. Trusting someone else might be more heartbreak than you're willing to risk. That was me. The thought of adding dating into this mix? The risk of getting my heart and my trust broken again? No thank you!

At least I knew exactly what the ache of aloneness felt like. I decided I'd rather live with this particular ache of what I knew than venture forward into what could possibly lead to even worse heartbreak. I had loving and supportive family and friends, I reminded myself. I hoped that in time, as I created a life alone, I'd be okay.

And I was . . . and I wasn't. I felt supported in my close relationships and protected in my isolation. But I also felt the ache of loneliness. So, as I wrote in this chapter, I began to entertain the idea of dating.

When others mentioned dating, initially just the thought of it made me panicky. What if I knew right away the match wasn't going to work, but I had to stay on the date a reasonable amount of time to not be rude? What if we had nothing to talk about? And what would my friends and family think? And how on earth do you date at this age?

And worst of all, what if I got my heart broken again? It felt like jumping out of a plane with no parachute. In fact, some days I would choose that over dating. But with reminders from friends of how much I'd healed, I took one baby step into the dating world. And that led to a series of steps: saying yes to a friend wanting me to meet her friend, downloading a dating app, and then . . . going on dates. Mercy.

I stumbled and fumbled and thought, *What in the world was I thinking?* But I also laughed and had fun and discovered some great guys. And in time, one great guy.

I learned that *What if it doesn't work out?* could be shifted to *What if it does?*

I'm a big believer in this happier version of the what-if question. This simple little question shifts my perspective away from my fears of having my trust broken again to embracing the path forward. It reminds me that while I can't rewrite my past, I also can't let it dictate my future. I can turn the page and write a new chapter. So what does your baby step look like? Reaching out with a short text? Inviting someone to coffee? Communicating what you need to feel safe in a relationship? Telling friends you're open to dating? Or a perspective shift: *I'm not going to say never.* Or *I'm not going to say I won't.*

Think about a baby learning to walk. First she learns to stand while holding on to her mother, who makes her feel safe. Then she lets go and stands. She takes one wobbly step, falls down, and goes back to crawling for a while. But she gets back up and tries again. And this time she takes more wobbly steps. And her parents cheer for her like they've never seen anyone walk before!

No one has ever said about a baby learning to walk, "She didn't do a very good job. She made a lot of mistakes. Maybe she shouldn't try walking." Right? We know that's ridiculous! But don't we do that to ourselves? We expect ourselves to move forward in trust perfectly, making no mistakes. And don't we often think God has that expectation too?

God, however, is our loving Father who holds us by the hand. Psalm 37:23–24 tells us, "The LORD directs the steps of the godly. He delights in every detail of their lives. Though they stumble, they will never fall, for the LORD holds them by the hand" (NLT). So let the Father hold your hand as you move forward, trusting that He won't let go till you're ready to stand. And when you do stand, He'll be right by your side.

Guided Journaling

1. After being a part of a couple for so long, I wasn't sure how to navigate being alone. You might be in a similar situation, or you might be trying to move forward in a different situation, but it is still new to you and makes you feel alone and awkward and scared and sad. I both didn't want to try again . . . and didn't want to be alone.

   Acknowledging that we can feel two opposite things simultaneously is helpful when we're healing. Write about some of the contrasting feelings you have.

   _____

   _____

   _____

   _____

   _____

   _____

   _____

   _____

   _____

   _____

2. After my divorce, I felt like somehow the divorce itself had not just made me feel intensely alone but had also diminished who I was and how people saw me. And maybe most tragically of all, how I saw myself. My friend Candace helped me see something important about labels and why I was struggling with divorce being part of my story. A friend who had cancer started to feel like every room she walked into she brought cancer with her. Instead of people seeing her, they saw cancer. I felt the same way with divorce. I didn't want "divorce" to be the first thing that people thought of when my name was mentioned. Divorce is a hard part of my story, but I didn't want it to so deeply mark me that it suddenly defined me.

How do you relate to this with some hard reality in your life? Also, what are some of the good parts of your story that shouldn't be forgotten and are more in keeping with who you really are?

_____

_____

_____

_____

_____

_____

_____

_____

_____

_____

_____

_____

_____

3. Some of my deepest grief was and still can be about losing the life I'd imagined. It's hard to move forward when what I really want is something from my distant past. Something that I can't reach. That I can't touch. But something that is still very alive in my memories. In my case, I didn't want to get back the person from my past. I wanted to get back the feeling of certainty about my future. I wanted to get back the feeling of knowing I had a person. I wanted to get back the feeling that I could trust a person to have my best interests in mind. I wanted to get back the feeling of safety that what this person had invested in our life together was enough, that they'd protect our vision because they wanted it as much as I did.

   We need to grieve the loss of those feelings of safety and security and our hopes and dreams for the future. What losses from the past and future are you grieving? You can use this prompt: I want back the feeling of . . .

   _____

   _____

   _____

   _____

   _____

   _____

   _____

4. When we are grieving broken trust, the "firsts" can be triggers. I remember the first time I was filling out some paperwork that required me to list my emergency contact. My chest tightened. My stomach clenched. I'd lost my emergency contact.

   Have you had triggering moments, maybe some of those "firsts," reminding you of your aloneness? Write those down. How did you respond? What change would you like to make in your response?

   _____

   _____

   _____

----

5. After a couple of years, people started asking, "When are you going to start dating?"
To most people I would say something vague, like, "Not yet" or "Maybe one day."
Eventually, without telling anyone, I began to explore the idea of dating, digging into
my thoughts and being honest with myself. And what I discovered surprised me a
bit: I was controlling. Me? I tended to go with the flow and to be easygoing.

But when it came to trusting someone with my heart, that was different. I knew
that if someone else got close enough to be known as my new person, I couldn't
control life nearly as much as I wanted to. When we have our trust broken, it's
really tempting to replace trust with control. If I can control it, I don't have to deal
with my trust issues. And when I say "control," I mean "do everything I can to
keep things as predictable as possible." If I can stay in control of situations, then
I falsely believe I can avoid the risk of trust.

In what ways do you think you may have become controlling?

----

6. Trust issues show up in so many ways, not just dating. Your next step forward may not be in the dating arena, but this plays out in other ways as well. At work, I don't have to trust that someone will do their job if I am micromanaging their tasks. In my friendships, I don't have to trust that I won't get disappointed or be a disappointment to someone if I keep our conversations from getting too deep and only get together with them occasionally. However this translates into your fears around trust, I want to validate how scary it can feel to trade the predictability we want for the risk of relationships with no guarantees.

    Where do you see yourself micromanaging? If you don't see that, let's explore this another way. Where do you see yourself resisting trust?

    _____

    _____

    _____

    _____

    _____

    _____

    _____

Along with control, there are other signs we are trying to eliminate or minimize the risk of trusting people. Put a check by any of the following symptoms that resonate with you right now.

☐ I become skeptical and suspicious of most people.
☐ I keep everything in and stuff my emotions.
☐ I tend to isolate and avoid relationships, telling myself I don't need anyone.
☐ I keep things light and surface-y in most relationships to avoid vulnerability.
☐ I avoid thinking about trust issues by numbing negative feelings with food, scrolling, streaming, shopping, alcohol, or drugs.

☐ I am good at listening to others but not at opening up to others.

☐ I get logical about a hurtful situation as a way to avoid looking inward.

☐ I blame myself.

☐ I deal with a violation of trust by saying, "I'm fine" or saying nothing at all.

☐ I get defensive and overreact.

☐ I overindulge.

☐ I overspiritualize.

☐ I keep outward life busy with things like overworking, overexercising, or oversocializing.

☐ I overthink and obsess.

☐ Something else?

_____

_____

_____

7. Sometimes our discernment will tell us this is not a safe person. This is not a place to try to move forward. At the same time, however, we must be honest with ourselves. Are we simply trying to create a no-risk situation? I know I've done that in self-protection. I wanted what felt predictable so badly that I was willing to miss out on all that might be possible.

What is your biggest fear when it comes to taking the risk of a close relationship? What are you afraid might or might not happen? Take some time to pray about this, to be honest with God and yourself. You can write your prayer and thoughts here. You can start with this prompt:

If I trust _____ (name), then I'm afraid . . .

_____

_____

_____

_____

_____

When we become insistent on certainty, change doesn't happen. Staying stuck happens. Protection and guardedness happen. But now, after time has passed and we've worked on healing, we are in a different place. I like the directness of Ecclesiastes 11:4 and how it can apply here: "If you wait for perfect conditions, you will never get anything done" (TLB). A reminder that if we define perfect conditions as no risk, then we are going to stay in the same place. Write down any thoughts you have about this.

---

8. When it came to dating, my wise and trusted friends thought I was ready. My counselor thought I was ready. But I wouldn't believe it for myself until I took a step. A baby step. A small declaration step where I stopped doubting my ability to make wise choices. What's your baby step? Remember, we don't need to move forward in big leaps. One increment at a time. Test the waters. Say, *We'll see.* But if you are ready to take a big leap, okay!

Maybe you'll start like I did with a perspective shift. For me, that was deciding not to say *never.* Another one for me was acknowledging that I could feel somewhat anxious—okay, sometimes a lot anxious—and move forward at the same time. Write the baby steps or big leap you plan to take here. Or write down ones you've already taken.

An unexpected result of my small steps forward was learning to have confidence in myself again. I didn't realize how much my confidence in making good decisions had diminished, and you may realize the same thing. But now you can move forward with experiential wisdom, healing from trust issues (not completely but significantly), and tools for making better decisions.

Action Steps

Today assess yourself to see where you're growing and healing and where you need to continue to grow.

A. Circle any of the feelings that apply when you complete this statement:

When it comes to trust, I feel . . .

anxious	weary	happy
hopeless	afraid	content
sad	cautious	confident
self-protective	regretful	comfortable
ashamed	peaceful	calm
doubtful	hopeful	_____
skeptical	eager	_____
angry	sure	_____

Are there feelings that you circled that you don't want to feel? Are there feelings you're thankful you feel? Any other observations?

_____

_____

_____

_____

_____

_____

_____

_____

B. I'm proud of myself for taking the following baby—or big—steps forward in trust.

_____

_____

_____

_____

_____

_____

_____

_____

_____

C. Think back to the previous chapters. Write three takeaways that have been most helpful to you.

_____

_____

_____

_____

_____

_____

_____

_____

_____

D. Think back to the previous chapters. Write three action steps you've taken as a result of moving forward in trust.

_____

_____

_____

_____

_____

_____

_____

_____

_____

E. At the beginning of this journal, we agreed that we'd approach journaling about our trust issues with compassionate exploration. How are you doing at extending yourself grace in this process?

_____

_____

_____

_____

_____

_____

_____

Scripture

The LORD directs the steps of the godly. He delights in every detail of their lives. Though they stumble, they will never fall, for the LORD holds them by the hand.

PSALM 37:23-24 NLT

When the clouds are full of water, it rains. When the wind blows down a tree, it lies where it falls. Don't sit there watching the wind. Do your own work. Don't stare at the clouds. Get on with your life.

ECCLESIASTES 11:3-4 MSG

Although the Lord has given you bread of deprivation and water of oppression, He, your Teacher, will no longer hide Himself, but your eyes will see your Teacher. Your ears will hear a word behind you, saying, "This is the way, walk in it," whenever you turn to the right or to the left.

ISAIAH 30:20-21 NASB

Playlist

"Dancing on the Waves," We the Kingdom

"I Have Decided to Follow Jesus," Phil Wickham

"Shattered," Blanca

Prayer

God, You know how sometimes I ache with aloneness. You've seen me grieve my losses, and although I know I'll still have sad moments, I want to move forward in trust. You know how afraid I am to try again and to hope again. Reveal to me where I turn to control or micromanaging instead of trust, or where I use other methods to try to self-protect. Help me to continue to heal so I can have the close relationships I long for. Help me to be brave in taking baby steps. Please bring into my life safe people I can connect with. Amen.

Chapter 6

How Can I Trust God When I Don't Understand What He Allows?

t's hard for me to start this story because I'm not ready to use my friend's name in past tense. She was a wonderful friend. She *is* a wonderful friend. And she passed away very quickly after a severe diagnosis. I think I'm still in disbelief because she was such a bright light in this world—in my world—that you can't extinguish all that goodness, joy, love, spunk, faithfulness, and unending hope.

I still want to call her and give her updates. We were in the middle of planning another trip together. We were in the middle of doing ministry work together. We were in the middle of processing my life finally taking a good turn after she'd prayed me through a decade of heartbreaks. She still had grandbabies being born and adventures she wanted to go on and so much wisdom she wanted to share with all of us.

And then right in the middle of all that life, an illness slammed the brakes on everything, and conversations were filled with words like *cancer* and *tumors* and *treatments* and prayers for a miracle.

But having all those hard conversations just wasn't in keeping with who Lisa was. Yes, we even shared the same name. In the first conversation we had after her diagnosis, she told me she only wanted to have joy conversations with me. So any conversations acknowledging this awful illness quickly changed to her asking me to tell her about a new turn in my life. A new love. After all, she was my friend who reminded me through all the really hard years leading up to and after my divorce, "You know, Lysa, God is the God of romance, and He's not going to leave you with a broken heart." And she believed that with all her heart. No wavering. No doubts. Only great anticipation for me. I had big doubts and big fears. So I would often roll my eyes and nervous laugh when she brought this topic up.

So you can imagine her absolute delight when I finally met and fell in love with Chaz.

She hadn't gotten to know Chaz before she got sick. Though we had been dating nearly a year, because we all lived in different towns, we hadn't all been in one place at the same time. But now she wanted to meet him with more urgency. So we made it happen.

The day they met was one I'll never forget. Lisa and I were in the middle of telling Chaz the story of her belief that God is the God of romance when suddenly, Chaz got down on one knee and proposed to me. Lisa and I were both in shock. And then we started laughing and hugging and taking lots of pictures.

That day was my first day of being engaged and my last day to be with my friend. As we hugged goodbye, Chaz captured that moment in a photo. She had the most beautiful look on her face, and it looked like she was gazing toward heaven. A few weeks later, she was watching a movie and eating ice cream when she took her last breath and stepped into heaven.

On my wedding day I carried that picture of us hugging tucked into my wedding vows wrapped around my bouquet. I miss her so much. I can't talk about her without crying. And as I process my grief, I've encountered more hard questions I have for God. Why her? Why this special person who brought such good into every life she touched? She

honored God with her whole heart and lived His love out in such beautiful ways. How could any of this be part of a good plan?

My wrestling is compounded by the unfairness of her life ending and others who cause such destruction and evil being physically healthy and free to keep hurting others. I know God is patient, wanting everyone to repent and turn from their sin. I believe His patience with all of us is part of His goodness.

And I hurt that my friend was taken.

I've made peace with the fact that I don't understand and I won't get answers to those questions. But I still cry, and I still wrestle with what seems so unfair to me. As we start with the guided prompts from this chapter, you may be struggling to understand something hard that God has allowed. Remember that God can handle all your thoughts and feelings, even your doubts and questions. I think this chapter of journaling will give you encouragement and tools to help you move forward in trusting God.

Guided Journaling

1. We all have belief systems about the way people should treat one another. And when someone's actions don't line up with that, we can be bewildered, frustrated, and hurt. These are two statements that we've all probably thought or said in these situations:

   I don't understand why that person did that.

   I wouldn't have done what they did.

   If it's helpful, write about some of the actions of others that have shocked you because you never thought they would do what they did or that they shouldn't have done what they did.

   _____

   _____

   _____

   _____

   _____

   _____

   _____

   _____

   _____

   _____

The reality is that there will always be a gap between what we see and the full story God knows.

2. I find that my thoughts about not understanding people often spill over into my thoughts about God. And I find myself thinking and praying things like,

    God, I don't understand why You would allow this. You could have stopped it. Why didn't You?

    God, this is wrong. This is so unfair. It doesn't seem like You're answering my prayer.

    What about you? What questions do you ask God?

    God, why did You _____?

    _____

    _____

    _____

    _____

    _____

    _____

    _____

    _____

    God, why didn't You _____?

    _____

    _____

    _____

    _____

    _____

Let's explore our fears about trusting God. For example, if I don't feel like God is coming through for me today, it's so hard to trust that surrendering my future to Him is a safe thing to do. I'm scared to fully trust Him. I'm scared to fully surrender my efforts to fix things and instead cling to His promises. So I hold on to my fears and doubts, and I build safety nets in case He doesn't come through. The reality is that there will always be a gap between what we see and the full story God knows. That gap is where so many of my fearful what-if questions come from as I look ahead and play out worst-case scenarios. What do you think of when you think of the gap between what you see and what God knows?

3. In the book, I provide a number of fill-in-the-blanks when it comes to our what-if questions. In the remainder of this chapter's journaling, I'm going to provide those same questions here. If you've already answered these in the book, revisit them to see where you've grown. For our first what-if question, let's address the fears tangled around our faith.

    a. What if I wrote down each thought of distrust so they don't all stay jumbled up inside me as big feelings of fear and anxiety?

- I fear trusting God with _____

  because He allowed _____

  _____ to happen in my past.

- I fear trusting God with _____

  _____ because if He doesn't come through for

  me in the way I want Him to, I will suffer _____

  _____.

- I fear trusting God with _____

  _____ because I don't think God will really _____

  _____.

- I fear trusting God with the suffering and heartbreak I'll go through if

  _____ happens, and I fear

  I won't ever _____.

b. What if expressing my true feelings to God is a beautiful act of trusting God?

The more I tried to bury my doubts, the uglier the doubts became. Acknowledging them instead of stuffing them down brought healing and new growth. How does this tie into trust? Well, leaning into doubt is an expression of trust in God. If I can trust God with doubts about Him, then I can trust Him with anything.

Explore your doubts about trusting God by filling in the blanks below.

- I sometimes doubt that God will _____

_____ because

_____.

- I feel _____

right now because God is (or isn't) doing _____

_____.

- What I really want to see happen is _____

_____.

- And if this doesn't happen, it will cause me to feel _____

_____.

- I don't want to feel _____

because I don't think I could handle _____

_____.

c. What if I looked at Scripture in a new way? Too often I read God's Word to try to make sense of what I'm facing. But what if the scriptures are really inviting us to see in part how God sees things? Read the following verses and respond to the prompt.

I will instruct you and teach you in the way you should go; I will counsel you with my loving eye on you.

PSALM 32:8

How does this verse help you look at what you're facing in a different way?

_____

_____

_____

_____

"The LORD does not look at the things people look at. People look at the outward appearance, but the LORD looks at the heart."

1 SAMUEL 16:7

How does this verse help you look at what you're facing in a different way?

_____

_____

_____

_____

_____

"Your Father knows what you need before you ask him."

MATTHEW 6:8

How does this verse help you look at what you're facing in a different way?

_____

_____

_____

_____

_____

_____

_____

_____

_____

_____

_____

_____

d. Suffering can shrink our perspective. When we feel pain, we can become fixated on addressing the source of the pain. We may think the only good move God could make is to take away the pain. And if that's all we are looking for, then we will become more frustrated and distrustful of God. But what if God's Word can help us see how to suffer and still be certain of His goodness? What if, instead of being so frustrated by what I don't see, I let God's Word be the lens through which I get to receive glimpses of His goodness that only those of us who suffer get to see?

Read the verses below, and use the prompt to journal after each one.

We also glory in our sufferings, because we know that suffering produces perseverance.

ROMANS 5:3

When I read this verse, I see suffering isn't just this awful pain. Suffering is also . . .

"When you pass through the waters, I will be with you; and when you pass through the rivers, they will not sweep over you. When you walk through the fire, you will not be burned; the flames will not set you ablaze."

ISAIAH 43:2

When I read this verse, I see suffering isn't just this awful pain. Suffering is also . . .

I remain confident of this: I will see the goodness of the LORD in the land of the living. Wait for the LORD; be strong and take heart and wait for the LORD.

PSALM 27:13–14

When I read this verse, I see suffering isn't just this awful pain. Suffering is also . . .

_____

_____

_____

_____

e. What if, instead of doubting God's goodness, I started cooperating with His goodness?

What does it mean to cooperate with God's goodness? It means to notice His goodness, to call it out, and to find calming enjoyment in those small evidences. Maybe we won't immediately see the big miracle we keep looking for. But we can see His goodness in other ways, right now, today.

This has become such a crucial aspect of my journey. When I don't see any good in a tough situation I'm going through, I think His goodness can only be evidenced by Him doing something to turn that situation around or at least something to assure me He's working on it. But I'm learning to expand my view and acknowledge His goodness in other places of my life. A lot of times it's the small stuff that I forget is a direct result of our good Creator God. Here are some examples of small stuff that help me remember the big reality of God's goodness:

- The sweetness of a perfectly ripe peach
- Music that calms my mind and makes me exhale
- The sun that comes out from behind a cloud and warms me on a chilly day
- Lights that are strung between backyard trees, hanging above a circle of friends around a firepit

- An unexpected but truly satisfying belly laugh
- The smell of morning coffee, my favorite flower, or my favorite dessert baking in the oven
- Watching the ocean waves on a gorgeous day go just so far and then pull back inside themselves

Write down some of the evidence of the goodness of God you're experiencing in small, everyday ways. Now write down who you could share this with or give this to. When we spread His goodness to other people, we are cooperating with His goodness to us.

_____

_____

_____

_____

_____

_____

f. What if our suffering is what actually reveals God's goodness in the most intimate and personal ways? Write down some ways you've personally experienced the goodness of God in the past.

- I felt God's goodness when He _____.

- Just the fact that I am _____ now is evidence of

  His goodness when I went through _____,

- I sometimes forget that _____ would never

  have happened in my life apart from the goodness of God.

g. What if I don't trust God? And, what if I do?

Can I bring about a good outcome on my own? Would that outcome come without challenges? Would that outcome require me to participate in the futile exercise of trying to change another person? Do I really have the ability to find stability and safety and peace and joy by going my own way?

_____

_____

_____

_____

_____

_____

_____

_____

_____

_____

_____

_____

Time for another deep breath. That's a whole lot to think through.

I'm going to end with us just sitting with those last questions. Usually I like my chapters to end with a big perspective change or with solutions to our problems and answers to our questions. But this isn't the chapter for that. This is weighty stuff. Ultimately, trusting God is holding loosely the parts of my life I want to hold most tightly. I want to trust Him until I don't. And that tension isn't one to solve. It's one to wrestle with well in this temporary place called now.

Action Steps

Option A:

You've been writing quite a bit, so if you need to take a break from that, try this: Light a candle. Play worship music from the playlist or songs you've been adding. Simply enjoy.

Option B:

Get a jar or box and decorate it in a way that makes you happy. Now on individual pieces of paper, write down some things that remind you of God's goodness or a prayer of thanksgiving, and put the papers in your container. Put this somewhere you can see it and add to it throughout the days to come. Periodically review your ideas and rejoice in God's goodness.

Scripture

But now, this is what the LORD says, He who is your Creator, Jacob, and He who formed you, Israel: "Do not fear, for I have redeemed you; I have called you by name; you are Mine! When you pass through the waters, I will be with you; and through the rivers, they will not overflow you. When you walk through the fire, you will not be scorched, nor will the flame burn you. For I am the LORD your God, The Holy One of Israel, your Savior."

ISAIAH 43:1–3 NASB

"Your Father knows what you need before you ask Him."

MATTHEW 6:8 NASB

Not only so, but we also glory in our sufferings, because we know that suffering produces perseverance; perseverance, character; and character, hope. And hope does not put us to shame, because God's love has been poured out into our hearts through the Holy Spirit, who has been given to us.

ROMANS 5:3–5

Playlist

"Crawl," Madison Ryann Ward and Aaron Gallard
"It Is Well with My Soul," Anthem Lights
"Thy Will," Hillary Scott & the Scott Family

Prayer

Heavenly Father, I get caught up in what I don't understand and let this fuel my distrust in You. Forgive me for that. Help me release my insistence on wanting to understand or wanting You to work out a situation the way I think You should. Today I choose to trust You with what I cannot see, do not know, do not want, and am afraid of. I hold loosely to outcomes and plans and hold tightly to You. In Jesus' name, amen.

Chapter 7

How Can I Trust God When the Person Who Hurt Me Got Away with It?

I'd been walking with one of my good friends through a divorce situation very similar to mine. We were trying to understand one of the worst days she'd had in this whole process. Some things happened that were the exact opposite of what we had prayed for and what we had believed for. This recent outcome seemed so unjust and unfair.

Sometimes I get nervous to pray really bold prayers, because then if the opposite happens—like in this situation—I question, *Was I praying the wrong thing, or is God just not listening?*

But I didn't let those questions hold me back from speaking a truth that came to me as we sat together praying and processing that day. I told her, "God's been so faithful to me throughout this journey, but sometimes I can't see it in the moment. I can, however, learn a lot when I look back and see what God did before. And today, I need to remember that what God did then He can also do now. And I need to ask myself, *What did I learn then that could give me the wisdom to handle what's going on now?*"

When I'm wrestling and trying to understand a situation, I've learned I have to stop and have this time of remembrance. And then I need to pray. And I mean really, *really* pray that God would show me what I need to do next, and that I would know that it is His voice leading me.

I told my friend this, and then I said, "I think we need to have a defined, marked moment of prayer right now and then get up and live in expectation over these next couple of days. God is going to reveal Himself and what should be done."

Later that day as I was driving home, I got an overwhelming sensation to look at my pictures from that exact day four years earlier in 2019. That had been an especially difficult year for me, so I didn't really want to do this because I was afraid of seeing photos that would bring back painful memories. But this prompting was very strong and very clear. I reminded myself that my friend and I had had this marked moment of prayer and were choosing to live in expectation of God revealing Himself, so maybe this was God prompting me.

When I got home and looked at my photos, I discovered I'd taken only one picture on April 17, 2019. It was a picture I'd taken on my property of the rose garden I'd planted, and next to it was an old shed that was falling apart. What's the significance of this picture? This is the exact spot where I'd begun to have a vision of building a special place of respite and compassion for those walking through deep relationship pain.

Now, years later, when I look at that spot, the rose garden is flourishing and next to it there's no longer a dilapidated shed. Instead, there's a dream come true. It's a beautiful white house with a tall roof, a welcoming patio, and space enough for me to gather groups of hurting women and offer them help.

As I stared at this picture, I thought about how God wanted me to see this "before" picture to compare to the picture I see now when I look out my front window at this exact same spot all these years later. Now I see what God did when the shed was torn apart and we were obedient to build something new.

What once felt so impossible, like an unrealistic dream, came to fruition. I was awe-struck by God.

This picture was evidence and such a powerful reminder that all the pain of my life being torn apart was not for nothing. The new building was a tangible way I could see my life becoming new. Instead of a remodel, it was a teardown and a new creation. The tear-down was crucial or else the new building wouldn't have a solid foundation and wouldn't turn out stable and beautiful. Not every part of the process was what I wanted or expected, but in time, I could see why it was so important to keep trusting God through all the ups and downs.

Anything we place in the hands of our good God will not be wasted. God's touch is life. God can take what was just a seed no one would notice in a pile of dirt and from it grow a rose garden. He can take the demolition of an old shed and make it holy ground where a haven can be built. He can take the mustard seed of our faith and in time grow our ability to trust Him beyond what we can imagine.

Through our obedience and trusting Him, we will see new growth and transfor-mation. Even in the situations that seem most unfair, like this very hard day for my friend. Even when it seems like the person who hurt you is getting away with something again. Even when it seems like your suffering might be pointless and that nothing good could come from it. God's view of things is higher and bigger and right in step with His faithfulness and goodness.

Anything we place in the hands of our good God will not be wasted.

What if you do what my friend and I did? In those situations you're facing right now where you want answers, but you don't have them; where you know God is working, but you can't see what He's doing; where His timing feels confusing, and you feel so discouraged. Can you commit to having a marked prayer time where you ask the Lord to clearly reveal Himself? Then get up from that prayer time and start living in expectation that He will absolutely reveal Himself. It might be in strange and unexpected ways like it was for me when I was suddenly overcome with the urge to look at old pictures. Whatever it is, look for the hand of God. He is right there with you.

I have to attach my hope to who God is. He is good. He is faithful. He is my Father, who loves me.

Guided Journaling

1. Some of the greatest feelings of betrayal I've felt occurred when I couldn't see any evidence of God intervening to help me or protect me. Big feelings led to big questions: "Where are You, God? Where is the part of my story where You fix things, right wrongs, and bring good from all of this? Where is the payoff for doing the right things? Where are the consequences for those doing the wrong things? Come on, God. What are You doing? I feel so alone and sad and distant from You."

   Journal about the questions and feelings that you relate to, and feel free to write your own big questions for God.

2. Feeling confused about what's happened to you, thinking about what God doesn't seem to be doing, and in turn fearing what else He might allow can become a focus or obsession that only leads to discouragement and doubting God. I finally realized I cannot attach my hope to God making things feel fair. And I certainly can't attach my hope to the outcomes I desperately want. I have to attach my hope to who God is. He is good. He is faithful. He is my Father, who loves me.

This is one of the biggest lessons I want you to take away from reading the book and journaling: Where we attach our hope changes everything. Where do you think you are attaching your hope?

Even now that I'm in a wonderful, loving relationship, I still have to do the same thing. I can't attach my hopes or happiness to this man or this good relationship. Even good humans are still fallible humans. That's true of all of us. So I still have to be careful where I attach my hope. Whether it's attaching your hopes to a certain outcome, a person, or something else, what have you discovered is the outcome of this?

_____

_____

_____

_____

_____

_____

_____

3. God's character that never changes is His personal promise to me. And to you. We can stand with assurance on who He is even when we don't understand what He does or doesn't do. Rather than attach our hopes to people or outcomes, we can hold on to the promises we find in His unchanging character.

Let's write as many characteristics of God as we can think of, turning to Scripture to help us. These truths can be a reminder to attach our hope to God's unchanging character. Here are some scriptures to get you started. Note which characteristic of God the verse illustrates. Then look up some more on your own.

How priceless is your unfailing love, O God! People take refuge in the shadow of your wings.

PSALM 36:7

God's characteristic: _____

The works of His hands are truth and justice; all His precepts are trustworthy.

PSALM 111:7 NASB

God's characteristic: _____

But when the kindness and love of God our Savior appeared, he saved us, not because of righteous things we had done, but because of his mercy.

TITUS 3:4–5

God's characteristic: _____

If we confess our sins, he is faithful and just to forgive us our sins and to cleanse us from all unrighteousness.

1 JOHN 1:9 ESV

God's characteristic: _____

Continue finding some more verses that correspond with God's character.

_____

_____

_____

_____

_____

_____

_____

_____

_____

4. When hard stuff continues to come our way for months and even years past the initial broken trust, it can feel like the fallout doesn't just affect our emotions. There are still ripple effects of deep grief. The hardships seem to have tentacles that reach out and touch every aspect of our life, and it's hard to fully step into the future when the past won't stay in the past. So much of what used to feel stable and sure now feels negatively impacted: children, finances, extended family, health, and friendships—and our ability to trust anyone, including God. When the fallout seems to keep going and going, it feels so unfair, exhausting, and disheartening.

What are the ripple effects you're experiencing right now?

_____

_____

_____

_____

_____

_____

_____

_____

Earlier in the journal I talked about how pain can get triggered in the most unexpected ways. Just the other day I ran into someone I hadn't seen since my divorce, and when they asked me questions about it, I felt so awkward. I wasn't sure what their intentions were, and it just felt icky. I was out running errands, but afterward I had no more energy for my day. I couldn't decide if I felt angry and defensive or just defeated and sad. Either way it triggered the heaviness of grief. How does grief show up for you? Are you allowing yourself to grieve?

_____

_____

_____

I don't know how you feel about crying, but I think sometimes you just need to cry to let out grief, sadness, frustration, and confusion. But some of us have a hard time crying. Maybe we've grown up that way or maybe we are simply too busy to indulge in that—or so we tell ourselves.

I remember a movie where the main character was in a taxi, and she sat there and cried hard for ten minutes. Then she wiped her eyes, stopped crying, and she was done for the moment. I remember that scene so well because it made so much sense to me. Sometimes you just need a good cry, and sometimes you don't have a lot of time because you have to carry on with life. What do you think about allowing yourself a designated time to cry when you feel the tears welling up in you?

----

5. In the book I wrote, "But if it was good for us to have this information, God would surely give it to us. So the fact that He isn't allowing us access to these specific details lets me know that having that information isn't what's best."

   I think it's profound to think about that first line—if God thought it would be good for us to know, then He would reveal it. I'm sure, like me, you've had why, how, and when questions for God about the things you want to have answers to but don't. If it's helpful, you can write those out here. We'll probably always have those types of questions, but I think we will default more quickly to acceptance when we remember that we have a good God who loves us. All His actions are filtered through that. What thoughts do you have about accepting what we don't understand?

   _____

   _____

   _____

   _____

   _____

   _____

   _____

   _____

   _____

   _____

6. For a variety of reasons, we can struggle to feel safe and settled when we don't have answers and don't understand why things are happening. Remember in chapter 2 I quoted my counselor: "The human brain is always in search of confidence in know-ing." Because of this, when you don't understand what God allows, are you more prone to fill in the gaps with negative assumptions or with hopeful trust in God? Maybe there are certain things that are easy for you to trust God with, but with

other things you struggle to trust Him. I can think of times when I didn't understand what was going on with a person, and as things unfolded in the future, some of my greatest fears came true. Do you sometimes wrestle with what God might allow to unfold in your future? Write your thoughts here.

_____

_____

_____

_____

_____

_____

_____

_____

_____

How does it help to remember that God doesn't work like humans do? He cannot lie. He keeps His promises, and His promises are always true. When have you felt confident of this?

_____

_____

_____

_____

_____

_____

Some days we wish God would show us a logical formula where if we do *x* and *y*, then we'll get *z*. That seems so much easier to deal with and a lot more predictable. However, God doesn't work in formulas. He works in relationships, and He works in a way that always lines up with His character. His relationship with each of us is based on His steadfast love. Here are some verses to remind you of how much God loves you.

How priceless is your unfailing love, O God! People take refuge in the shadow of your wings.

PSALM 36:7

The LORD is good to all; he has compassion on all he has made.

PSALM 145:9

Humble yourselves, therefore, under God's mighty hand, that he may lift you up in due time. Cast all your anxiety on him because he cares for you.

1 PETER 5:6–7

We know and rely on the love God has for us. God is love. Whoever lives in love lives in God, and God in them.

1 JOHN 4:16

Being confident of God's love for us changes everything. And that's what we need to fill our minds with. That's the thing we need to be confident in knowing. God loves us because of who He is and because we're His. He chose to love you and me, and He will never stop. How does shifting your focus to being confident of God's love affect your trust level with Him?

_____

_____

_____

_____

---

7. This is a reality that can be hard to swallow: We may never see the justice we long for on this side of eternity. Some will. But many will not. I can't explain this, but I'm working hard to accept it. Accepting this reality can be a lot to think about, process, and write about. So if you find yourself resisting, questioning, or feeling sad or mad about this, don't be surprised. You can write about that here.

Some things that have helped me accept this truth are:

- growing in my relationship with Jesus by seeking Him purposefully in prayer and being immersed in His Word
- processing with a friend who loves God, too, and who will **empathize**, listen, or give me solid feedback if that's what I need
- reading stories or listening to podcasts of faithful people
- spending time in person with a friend who has faithfully followed Jesus in hard times

I've learned to have a marked prayer time where I ask the Lord to clearly reveal Himself. Then I get up from that prayer time and start living in expectation that He will absolutely reveal Himself. Can you adopt some of these practices or choose some others when you are processing hard realities? Write your ideas or your prayers here.

_____

_____

_____

_____

_____

_____

_____

_____

_____

_____

_____

_____

8. A deep hurt I experienced was in regard to an article that was published uncovering some of the details of my divorce. I was never contacted to verify the facts. And then other media outlets picked up the article and published it. It hurt so much that these were *Christian* media outlets. I want to acknowledge that the hurt from Christians especially stings. I've had Christians question me as if they doubt what I experienced was as serious as it was. And some Christians seemed eager to heap condemnation on me. How has gossip or speculation or judgment ever added to your deep hurt and skepticism about trusting people?

_____

_____

_____

_____

_____

_____

_____

_____

Maybe a person, ministry, or church has said or done something to make you feel like you can't trust other Christians. Maybe you've stopped going to church, withdrawn from other Christians and fellowships, or stopped supporting a ministry because you've grown distrustful. Write about that, as well as the ways you have been able to keep your heart soft even when you've been mistreated.

_____

_____

_____

_____

_____

_____

_____

_____

_____

_____

9. Eventually, one of the truths that helped me—and still helps me manage the unfairness of hurtful situations—is that when people sin against us, they unleash into their lives the consequences of that sin. We may never see it. In fact, it may look like they just got away with everything. But today we can be reminded that eventually "they will eat the fruit of their ways and be filled with the fruit of their schemes" (Proverbs 1:31).

As we approach the end of this chapter of journaling, I wonder how you feel about this question now: How can I trust God when the person who hurt me got away with it? How does the above verse help you have confidence that you can trust God with justice?

_____

_____

_____

_____

_____

_____

_____

_____

10. We can be tempted to do the wrong thing in hard situations that seem unfair, to take into our own hands righting the wrong. We've probably each been there or will be there at some point. Someone will be untrustworthy. We'll want to spew anger and hurt and possibly revenge. Maybe you've done this in the past. But what a sad thing that would be if we let the other person have more power over us. They've taken so much from us; let's not let them take any more. The best thing we can do is trust God with their consequences while making sure we don't get lured into sinful choices trying to right the wrongs.

Remember, it is good for us to confront the wrongdoings of others and address sins committed against us. But sometimes this desire to right certain wrongs can turn into something more. Have you been rehearsing ways in your mind that you could give them a taste of their own medicine? Or does the thought of something bad happening to them make you want to have a little celebration in your heart? I get it. But I also know that that won't make things better for you, and it could possibly validate ugly things people have said about you. Once when a friend knew she was going to run into a family member that deeply hurt her, I told her, "Prove them wrong. Don't validate their worst thoughts of you. Prove them wrong."

That thing you're thinking about doing or the angry words you're thinking about texting? Decide now you're not going to do it and write your declaration here. Tell God you'll obey Him and trust Him with the outcomes.

_____

_____

_____

_____

_____

_____

_____

_____

And maybe, like me, you have said some things you know you shouldn't have. Or maybe you have retaliated in ways you now wish you hadn't. If you have sin to confess, do that now too. Remember, God is ready to forgive you. God understands. But God also wants us to let Him take vengeance. Write what's on your heart here.

_____

_____

_____

_____

_____

_____

_____

_____

_____

11. My friend Jenny is mature in her faith and is one of the most gracious and sup-portive people I know. She shared that even though she is truly happy when others' prayers have been answered, sometimes it can be a struggle when she's still waking up to hard and heartbreaking things each day.

She explained that she had an epiphany about how to better manage other people's celebrations while she's still hurting. I knew it was a game changer for my perspective as well. Jenny said, "Their path to see God's glory is different than mine." Think about this phrase and journal about how it can help you shift your perspective.

_____

_____

_____

Another phrase that has helped me is "This is not my forever."

Write down these or other helpful phrases and then display them where you can see them daily. Practice using these phrases in those hard moments. You can even turn them into a prayer: *God, I know this is not my forever, and I trust You.*

Action Steps

Option A:

Go outside! Or if you can't get outside, look at pictures of God's creation to see His tangible work in nature. Add some pictures of nature to your Moving Forward folder. You might want to play some of the worship songs suggested in this journal. I noted in this chapter that when I'm wondering where God is, His creation always seems to have a message about Him, if I pay close enough attention. If I can't see the work of His hands the way I thought I would in my circumstances, I want to see His work somewhere.

Option B:

Choose some of God's characteristics you want to focus on. Then collect a group of objects to represent these characteristics and display them somewhere easily visible. Be creative! Think about pictures, colors, written or printed Scripture verses, everyday objects from inside your home or from nature. For example, you could include a photo of a friend who reminds you of God's trustworthiness; a framed verse to remind you of God's faithfulness; a book to reflect God's wisdom; a rock to represent God's power. Take a picture and add this to your Moving Forward folder.

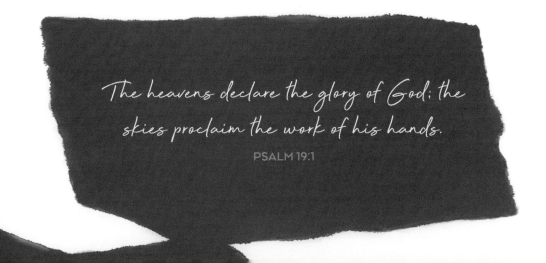

The heavens declare the glory of God; the skies proclaim the work of his hands.

PSALM 19:1

Scripture

Take care, brothers and sisters, that there not be in any one of you a wicked, unbelieving heart [which refuses to trust and rely on the Lord, a heart] that turns away from the living God. But continually encourage one another every day, as long as it is called "Today" [and there is an opportunity], so that none of you will be hardened [into settled rebellion] by the deceitfulness of sin [its cleverness, delusive glamour, and sophistication].

HEBREWS 3:12–13 AMP

They will eat the fruit of their ways and be filled with the fruit of their schemes.

PROVERBS 1:31

The heavens declare the glory of God; the skies proclaim the work of his hands.

PSALM 19:1

Playlist

"Be Still My Soul," Kari Jobe

"Good Good Father," The Worship Initiative, Shane & Shane

"Still in Control," Mack Brock

Prayer

Heavenly Father, I choose today to trust You with justice. In the situations that seem most unfair; with the person who seems to be getting away with their wrong choices; when I'm weary with suffering that never seems to end, I trust in Your faithfulness and goodness. When I'm tempted to hurt the other person or to take justice into my own hands, at that very moment, I choose to trust You're working even when I can't see what You're doing. I choose to look for You in other ways and places. Forgive me for the ways I take matters into my own hands, and give me trust to live surrendered to You. Thank You for being my good, good Father who loves me. Amen.

Chapter 8

What We Don't Trust We Will Try to Control

A friend told me a story about a hike she took in her twenties. One winter day she and a group of her friends bundled up in hats and mittens, drove to a nearby national park, checked out the posted map, and hit the trail for what would be a three-hour hike.

Three hours?! she thought. What in the world. She loved the mountains but was more the type to look at the scenery from the comfy-cozy couch in front of the fireplace. But she didn't want to be the only one staying at the house, so she joined in. About an hour into the hike, she began to think, *I've had enough of this hiking stuff.* Her feet were sore, her nose was running, and she was seriously questioning the fun factor.

She'd been lagging behind everyone else. In fact, she couldn't even see the rest of the group. She had an epiphany: What if she found a shortcut to get to the end of the hike? Or better yet, what if she created her own shortcut? Surely going straight down the mountain would be shorter than the winding trail, right? So without telling her friends, she left the trail and started hiking down the mountain. Sure, forging her own trail was more difficult and time consuming than she imagined. She slid down the mountain some and got scratches from the prickly bushes, but she was doing it. She was forging her own trail, and she was sure she'd end up right where she wanted to be—the parking lot where they started out. She'd get in the car, turn on the heat, and rest until everyone else got there.

After a very long hike on her own trail, she ended up on a dirt road—in the middle of nowhere. This was way before cell phones, so calling for help was not an option. With no idea what to do, she started walking in what she hoped was the right direction. The dirt road eventually led to a highway. Again, she had no other choice but to pick a direction and hope for the best.

But the best didn't happen. She walked and walked. The sun got lower, and her anxiety got higher. Tears of fear and shame filled her eyes. Finally, a car pulled over and the driver asked if he could help her. Was he going to kidnap her, or worse? But what other choice did she have? She explained she needed to get to a certain parking lot, and he agreed to take her. She got in the car, said thank you, and put her hand on the door handle in case she needed to make an emergency escape.

After a short drive and as the sun was beginning to set, they pulled into the parking lot where her friends and a park ranger were grouped together. She leapt out of the car; her friends ran to her and hugged her tight. "Where have you been? We thought someone or something got you! What happened?" they asked. She cried, explained, apologized, and felt immense relief to finally be with her people again.

And she learned that in the future, she'd stay on the trail.

When my friend told me this story, I was shocked to hear she tried to forge her own trail down a mountain. But metaphorically, I've done the same thing. Don't we all make choices to forge our own trails? When situations are not what we expect or hope for. When our anxiety skyrockets because things aren't going the way we thought they would. When we're afraid. When we think of getting hurt again. When we fear we can't trust someone we once thought would never betray us. When God does the opposite of what we've prayed for. When it feels like more hard things just keep happening even though we are trying our best to honor God with our decisions.

These are the times when we face a crucial choice: Stay on God's path or forge our own trail? Follow God or rely on ourselves? One of the natural and understandable responses to broken trust is to want to take matters into our own hands and to try to control a person or situation. Being controlling can seem like the quickest way to reestablish safety and prevent what we are afraid will happen.

However, control rarely delivers what we want it to in the long run. Like my friend forging her own trail. She was in control, but the result wasn't her desired outcome.

So what do we do? We choose to trust, we choose to surrender, we choose to follow God on His path. Instead of filling the gaps of the unknown with our suggestions to God, we choose to put our trust in Him. We resolve to seek Him and to follow Him rather than trying to figure it all out and control it ourselves.

I love Psalm 23 for many reasons, and one of those is the promise that we have a loving Shepherd we can trust to lead us. Psalm 23 reads, "The LORD is my shepherd; I shall not want. He makes me lie down in green pastures. He leads me beside still waters. He restores my soul. He leads me in paths of righteousness for his name's sake" (1–3 ESV).

You might be thinking, *Lysa, you don't understand. You don't know what a hard path I'm on. How could God lead me here?* Oh, friend, I do understand. I've been on such rough paths I could hardly believe what my life had become. I've done exactly what I'm suggesting to you. Not perfectly, but even when I strayed from God's path, I made the choice to come back. No, it's definitely not easy. But we take one step at a time. We pray, *Lord, I'm surrendering this unexpected event to You. I feel like I want to take control and try to protect myself. But You are my Shepherd, and I choose to trust You.*

Then He shows us the next step to take on the path He's leading us on. We'll want to see many steps ahead or even all the steps ahead. What's this path going to look like? What will it lead to? Is it going to be easier or get more difficult? Is it going to lead to more unexpected places? We'll want more answers. But we'll remember, *The Lord is our Shepherd; we shall not want.* This is what trust looks like.

Guided Journaling

1. One of the dangers of being controlling is that we end up depending on ourselves, not on God. Yes, relying on ourselves in the sense of having confidence in our abilities to pray, discern, make wise decisions, and take action is a good thing. There can be a good side to being in control, especially if we've been insecure or passive in the past. But when taken to an extreme, we can become overly self-reliant, the opposite of God-reliant. Remember, controlling others isn't going to bring about the life we want. The illusion of control makes big promises but will never deliver.

   How have you held on to the illusion of control? What about letting go of control scares you? What about trusting God and being dependent on God scares you?

   As you identify your fears about trusting God, you might want to revisit the previous chapter (see question #3) and journal some more about God's character.

2. One of the areas I see so many of us trying to exert control is that of our closest relationships. Our motives might seem good, such as protecting them from harm, but in the end, our attempts to control often don't give us the outcome we want.

   A friend told me her adult daughter Rachel is in a relationship in which she sees all kinds of red flags. She's seen Rachel make a bad decision about a relationship in the past, so it's hard for her to trust her daughter's decisions now. She loves her daughter and simply wants to protect her from hurt. She's talked to Rachel, shared some of her concerns, but her daughter says she's grown and can make her own decisions. In desperation, my friend started to point out every negative quality she saw in this guy, and soon that's all she was talking to her daughter about. Now her daughter has been distancing herself. My friend loves her daughter, and it's so hard to see her make a decision that seems so unwise. It's not easy to *not* control, right? How do you relate to this situation?

If we think we are the stabilizing force keeping everything together and everyone else in line, we will be exhausted and disillusioned by people's imperfections. And we will fret and worry and possibly even have panic attacks when we recognize much safer routes in life but the people we love refuse to take them. *Exhausted, fretful, worried, panicky*: how can you relate to these words?

Which people do you find yourself trying to control? For each person you identify, write down why you think you try to control them. In other words, what are you trying to cause to happen or not happen?

You might want to use these prompts:

If I trust God with the situation with _____ (name of person),

then she/he might _____.

If I trust _____ (name of person) to figure out that

situation without giving my advice, then I'm afraid _____

_____.

If I trust _____ (name of person) to do

_____

but I don't see them doing that, then I'm afraid the consequences of their

actions will affect me, and I'll have to pick up the pieces.

If I trust _____ (name of person) to do

_____

but I don't see them doing that, then I'm afraid their actions will have deva-

stating consequences in their lives.

If the prompts don't apply or if you want to expand, you can write more here.

_____

_____

_____

_____

_____

_____

_____

_____

_____

_____

3. I wrote in the book about being caught off guard at a big event where I was speaking. While I can laugh about that now and acknowledge that being embarrassed is fairly harmless, being caught off guard with trust issues can be a much bigger deal with much more hurtful and painful impacts. These can be some of the hardest places to trust God: A friend throws you under the bus at work. Family members talk about you behind your back and assume the worst about you. A boyfriend or husband is unfaithful. A business partner siphons thousands from your co-owned business. A pastor is exposed as an alcoholic, addict, or adulterer. Your child makes an irresponsible choice that has detrimental consequences. You are misunderstood when you draw healthy boundaries.

Is there a specific situation that you fear will catch you off guard? What do you think is the root cause of the fear?

4. It's important to remember that humans who break our trust do not have the power to break apart God's good plans. People are never more powerful than God. While there will always be gaps in the trust we have with people, there are no gaps in the trustworthiness of God.

   There have definitely been times when it seems like people are powerful, haven't there? They've had the power to break our hearts, rattle our ability to trust, and cause us to guard ourselves to prevent more damage. In what ways have people seemed powerful in your life when it comes to broken trust?

   _____

   _____

   _____

   _____

   _____

   _____

   _____

   _____

   What does this last part—"There are no gaps in the trustworthiness of God"— mean to you?

   _____

   _____

   _____

   _____

5. How does relying on God's trustworthiness change you? You can use these prompts or write your own. Check the ones most important to you right now.

It will help me . . .

- ☐ stay calm when I'm caught off guard
- ☐ not overthink or become obsessive
- ☐ feel emotionally sound
- ☐ feel mentally stable
- ☐ not become controlling
- ☐ not feel so rattled by unexpected hard situations
- ☐ manage disappointments
- ☐ not get so worried or anxious or fearful about the future
- ☐ pray instead of worry
- ☐ keep my heart soft toward others and God
- ☐ not blow things out of proportion
- ☐ stop my thoughts from instantly jumping to worst-case scenarios
- ☐ trust others going forward
- ☐ trust the discernment I have
- ☐ trust God more easily in the future because I've seen His faithfulness

Add any other thoughts about relying on God's trustworthiness.

_____

_____

_____

_____

_____

_____

_____

6. The biggest of all risks in this journey is not that we will risk trusting and possibly have our hearts broken again. It's that we won't grow and heal from what happened.

    Just a reminder to both of us—moving forward is brave work. It's much easier to stay guarded, bitter, and untrusting. It's much more comfortable not to practice self-reflection, to give up on journaling, to give up on growing and healing. But you're making the brave choice!

    While I was working on this chapter, my friend was having a hard day, feeling emotional and triggered by old photos she'd stumbled across of her former marriage. She couldn't see the ways she'd moved forward, and maybe you can relate to this. Don't let one bad day fool you into thinking you haven't made any steps forward.

    I said to her, "You're purging years of heartbreak to make room for new possibilities. You're doing better than you think." You, too, might need to take these words to heart, friend. You can also ask a friend to help you identify ways you've grown in trust. In what ways can you see yourself growing, healing, and being able to look forward to the future?

    _____

    _____

    _____

    _____

    _____

    _____

    _____

    _____

    _____

    Take some time to celebrate growth and healing when it comes to trust. My friends and I often have our own little dance party around my kitchen table with the music blaring. Have fun celebrating any way you want to!

7. When facing each day with the good, the not so good, and the horrible, I am learning to have a posture of surrender. Remember, we are in the process of unlearning some tendencies and replacing those with practices that will enable us to rely on God. Surrendering is something we can learn and practice, even if imperfectly. Surrendering is what moves us from self-reliance to God-reliance. Write your own definition of surrendering.

_____

_____

_____

_____

_____

_____

_____

_____

_____

Especially in situations where we recognize that we're becoming controlling, we can immediately start to pray a prayer of surrender. One of the simplest prayers of surrender is this: "God, You lead, and I'll follow."

These are some more examples of prayers of surrender.

God, I'm surrendering this unexpected turn of events. Instead of panicking and missing Your provision, I'm going to look for Your provision that is here.

God, I'm surrendering this tension with my friend. Instead of rushing to make judgments against her or myself, I'm going to let the Jesus in me talk to the Jesus in her through prayer before addressing this issue.

God, I'm surrendering my doubts that You are really going to come through for me this time. Instead of looking at today's circumstances as evidence of Your absence, I'm going to trust that today is a necessary part of the process only You can see right now.

God, I'm surrendering how sad I feel today. Instead of trying to numb out in unhealthy ways, I'm going to get myself somewhere I can worship, listen to Your truth, look for Your presence in nature, or process this with people who are biblically wise.

Pray right now for God to reveal where you are trying to control and where you instead need to surrender. Pray one of the above prayers of surrender or modify it and make it your own. Praying with your hands open can be a sign of your surrender. You can write your prayer here.

8. I want to slow down and acknowledge how tough it is to release some of the ways we control, because honestly, our motivation isn't that we always want to be in charge but, rather, we want to be safe. I'm learning to acknowledge what may or may not happen in the future and still make the choice to live in today. This is what I can control: making wise choices right now, knowing God is in full control. This is what I can't control: all that happens in the tomorrows to come.

What does it look like for you to focus on making the choice to live in today?

_____

_____

_____

_____

_____

_____

_____

_____

_____

_____

_____

_____

_____

_____

_____

_____

Action Steps

In the book I suggested several action steps related to surrendering, so I'll include them here. Let these become part of your everyday prayers.

Surrendering looks like . . .

- Whispering a short surrender prayer to God: *God, You lead, and I'll follow.*
- Praying with my hands open.
- Writing down the individual things I'm worried about on index cards and laying them all out on the floor. The ones I can realistically work on, I pick up. All the others, I tuck into my Bible.
- Setting a short time limit on my swirling thoughts when I'm trying to figure things out and I start to obsess and worry. I'll give myself ten minutes more, and then I'll change my environment and tell myself, *I've done my part for today. Now I'll let God do His part for today.*

You might play worship songs from the playlist while you do any of the suggested activities.

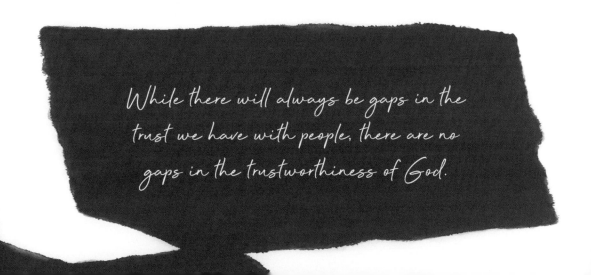

While there will always be gaps in the trust we have with people, there are no gaps in the trustworthiness of God.

Scripture

The LORD is my shepherd, I will not be in need. He lets me lie down in green pastures; He leads me beside quiet waters. He restores my soul; He guides me in the paths of righteousness for the sake of His name.

PSALM 23:1–3 NASB

Through the LORD'S mercies we are not consumed, because His compassions fail not. They are new every morning; great is Your faithfulness.

LAMENTATIONS 3:22–23 NKJV

"So don't worry about tomorrow, for tomorrow will bring its own worries. Today's trouble is enough for today."

MATTHEW 6:34 NLT

Playlist

"Carry You," Amy Grant

"Psalm 23," Shane & Shane

"Trust in God," Elevation Worship, featuring Chris Brown and Isaiah Templeton

Prayer

Heavenly Father, I continue to release hurts from past broken trust, and any unhealthy ways of dealing with them that I might be hanging on to in self-protection. When I fear the unknown future, I know one of my tendencies is to become controlling. Help me recognize when I'm doing this and to replace control with surrender to You. I want to follow, trust, and depend on You in every situation I find myself in, one day at a time. Help me hold loosely to people and outcomes and to hold tightly to You. Amen.

Chapter 9

Ice Makers and Oceans

We've journaled and worked hard and prayed and cried and rejoiced. We've been honest with ourselves and God. We've held tightly in fear, and we've let go in trust. We've let time pass, and we've worked on our trust issues. We've taken baby steps and big leaps forward. We've practiced new ways of thinking and doing. And we're not who we were when we first began journaling about moving forward in trusting others, God, and ourselves.

As we near the end of this journal, let's take time to celebrate our healing and our growth.

Like me, maybe you thought you'd never get to a better place. We thought brokenness, distrust, hurt, and fear would be written on every page of our stories. But that's not what God wrote for us. Traces of God's love mark every page of our stories. And because we are His, we've leaned into Him and learned to trust Him.

And here we are. Better than okay.

Friend, you and I are stronger and wiser and braver than we ever knew we could be. We're not just better than okay. We're our best *ever*. Let's celebrate our journey with the following poem:

What does healing and trusting again look like?
It looks like tears
Facing fears
Crawling back in bed
Covers over my head
It looks like time
Admitting I'm not fine
Not yet and no clue when
Wanting to give up
But not giving up
It looks like a fight
Staring up at midnight
A cold bed
Jumbled thoughts
Emotions both numb and wild
Deciding to live
Refusing to give . . . over to defeat
It's not a checklist
Or a clenched fist
Or an attempt to barely exist
No, healing is living
It's rebellious acts of resilience
It's chasing the sun
Rediscovering fun
It's climbing back up
Maybe clawing my way up

And through

And out

Refusing to entertain defeating doubt

It's working through what I'm walking through

And when another person breaks my trust

I won't let it break me

It's counseling and pondering

It's being okay with quiet

And then dancing it out so loudly

Lifting my head proudly

Kneeling to God humbly

And finally knowing I will be okay

Better than okay

Maybe my best ever

Definitely my best ever

Guided Journaling

1. In this chapter of the book, I shared a story about the time when the ice maker broke and I couldn't find a repairman to help me. I started spiraling. I was having an out-of-proportion reaction to the minor situation in front of me. And when that happens, I know it's not just about the thing. It's all the other things attached to this thing. I could feel the tears coming. Have you had an out-of-proportion reaction to a minor situation? One that reminded you of losses, betrayals, or aloneness? We've talked about triggers, but the reality is, triggers may keep occurring. Remember, healing is not a one-and-done event.

   Maybe you still feel mad or sad that life is not what you thought it would be, and you're not sure you can do the new life. In that moment I vented and blamed someone else and myself before I got to a better place. So go ahead and vent. Unfiltered.

You can use some of these prompts if they fit:

They should have _____.

If only I'd _____.

If only they'd _____.

It's not fair _____.

The hardest thing about right now is _____.

2. Continue some of those thoughts and what you believe as a result now.

Because I didn't _____,

I now have to deal with _____.

Because they did _____,

I now can't _____.

Because _____ happened,

I will no longer _____.

Journal any other thoughts you have about this.

_____
_____
_____
_____

3. As we move forward in trust, we are unlearning some things and learning new thought patterns and action steps that will help us move forward. Sometimes our moving-forward process is two steps forward, one step back. And some stumbling steps. Sometimes it's standing still. Don't berate yourself if you feel you're making missteps in this journey. Moving forward imperfectly is still moving forward.

   Along with the tangible evidence of acts of resilience, like fixing the ice maker, I began to adopt a new mindset: *Just because I've been hurt doesn't mean I have to live hurt.* What does living hurt mean to you, and how has that played out in your life? How does this quote challenge you or inspire you?

   _____

   _____

   _____

   _____

   _____

   _____

4. When you have your trust broken, part of what feels so incredibly unfair and hard to get through is how much it takes from you. Broken trust diminishes relationships, opportunities, the feeling of freedom you once felt when things seemed safe and secure. Skepticism starts to set in, not just with the person who broke your trust but with other people as well. What has broken trust taken from you? Maybe some of the things I listed? Others? What do you want to reclaim?

   _____

   _____

   _____

   _____

   _____

   _____

5. Another thing that happens when trust has been broken is that we put limitations on ourselves because of another person's actions. Can you identify any limitations you've put on yourself? Think of vows or proclamations where you've said things like, "I will never trust a man again." Or "I'm just not the kind of person who needs friends. I've had too many bad experiences and I've been hurt." Write any of those declarations you've said that limit the possibilities for your future.

    Search your heart to see if those declarations are things you really mean or are things you're saying as a way to self-protect. This was hard for me because I kept trying to convince myself those limiting statements were true, and I didn't want to be pushed into admitting otherwise. But a way that I turned the question to help me answer it more truthfully was this: If I knew I wasn't going to get hurt, would I still make these same declarations? What does this question reveal to you?

    ----

6. Has broken trust caused you to focus on what you've lost? In our journaling we've reflected on past events that have affected our trust. This prayerful self-reflection has been needed, as it's part of the healing process. Now let's focus on moving forward. These prompts will help you get started, and you can add more of your own.

- I think I might be too focused on _____

  _____.

  Taking my focus off this will help me move forward.

- I'm holding on to unforgiveness of _____ (person's name)

  about _____

  _____ (event that broke trust).

  I don't want to be bitter or unforgiving, so I'm surrendering this to God.

- I think I've been afraid to hope for good things in the future. Today I'm going

  to hope for _____

  _____.

- Lord, Your Word says when we trust You, You will bring good out of all

  things. Help me see the good. I'm thankful for _____

  _____

  _____ in this new season.

- Even though I've healed so much, I know I still need to get unstuck from

  _____

  _____.

- I haven't dreamed much about the future because I've been so focused on

  the past. Today I'll take time to dream. I imagine myself _____

  _____.

- I've been afraid or hesitant to do _____

  _____,

  but I'm going to do it _____

  _____ (when, time, and place).

7. A therapist who has done a lot of research on healing trauma said, "Trauma isn't an event that happens. It's how you process the event."[3] So if you process it in a healthy way, with a strong support system that helps you heal and see the truth more clearly, then the lasting effects won't be as devastating. But if you don't have that help as you experience a traumatic event, then you could end up feeling stuck in that trauma.

   I wrote about the long season I kept silent and the effect it had on me, and I believe because I kept silent about what was happening and had no one to process with and to receive care from, the trauma stuck with me. How does that resonate with you?

   I know I've referred to the importance of trustworthy friendships before—and I'm doing it again because it's difficult to heal in isolation.

Who have you invited in to help you carry what you're going through? Or if you haven't done this, can you choose to share with a safe person now?

_____

_____

_____

_____

_____

_____

_____

_____

_____

8. The story of betrayal wasn't just an event in my life. It became the story that messed up my life. Suffering and pain can shrink our perspective, and we can become fixated on fixing our pain. That's one reason we end up focusing on the story that messed up our lives. What's the story you've told yourself about the situation that rattled your trust?

_____

_____

_____

_____

_____

_____

Have you let that story overtake your thoughts and distort reality? If you're not sure, consider if you've done some of these things:

- You ask others about the person who hurt you. You're looking for how their life is turning out, hoping they're unhappy and their life is not turning out well.
- You look at their social media way too much.
- You lose sleep overthinking this issue.
- You keep trying and trying to understand their actions, and though you can't, you continue to fixate on it.
- You talk and talk and talk about this person or situation, possibly wearing out your supportive person.
- You avoid praying about the situation or person because you have a feeling God might want you to do something you're not doing and are maybe not willing to do.

Do you see yourself reflected in any or several of these statements? Which ones?

_____

_____

_____

_____

_____

_____

_____

_____

_____

Maybe you weren't ready to let go of a certain story, but I hope journaling has helped you get to a different place. Now you're ready to look at events through a new lens. Write about the ways you can look at that event differently. And remember, no part of this exercise is meant to diminish the pain it caused you or make you feel ashamed for not being ready to move forward previously. This is a place where you can acknowledge it but not get defeated by it.

_____

_____

_____

_____

_____

_____

_____

_____

_____

9. In the book I shared how that moment in the kitchen when I rebelled against the brokenness and fixed that ice maker taught me something big. And I just knew this rebellious act of resilience was going to be an important part of helping me move forward. Look up or write your own definition of resilience.

_____

_____

_____

_____

_____

I bet you've already done something as a rebellious act of resilience. Maybe you didn't call it that or maybe you didn't acknowledge it at the time. It can be the smallest thing. Some days getting out of bed and showering was a victory. I can think of several times when I didn't say the mean words I was thinking out loud to anyone. Instead, I prayed about it. Another day getting some paints and a canvas and creating something beautiful made me feel strong and alive and more me. What are some of your rebellious acts of resilience?

_____

_____

_____

_____

_____

_____

_____

10. Two words that indicated stuck-ness to me were "can't" and "don't."

I can't deal with this. I can't do this. I can't trust people. I can't fix this. I can't change. I don't think this is ever going to get better. I don't want to try. I don't believe it's possible. I don't think God has a good plan for me.

Make a list of the "can'ts" and "don'ts" you've found yourself thinking or saying.

_____

_____

_____

_____

_____

_____

11. Healing from betrayal and trust issues will be layered and can be complicated. It will take time. Probably more time than any of us will want it to. But by listening for our "I can'ts" and "I don'ts" and making sure they don't turn into "I won'ts," we can see significant progress today.

    Maybe try using some new words like *I am willing to try. Maybe I can find someone who can teach me. This is an opportunity for me to be brave. I can do this.* Or, like me, *But what if I could?* My counselor loves to remind me that words frame our reality. If we believe we can't, chances are we won't.

    What thoughts do you have about saying "I won't"? Can you think of times when saying this has held you back from moving forward? Write down several of your "I won't" statements.

    _____

    _____

    _____

    Which ones can you turn into "I can" or "I will consider" or maybe "I could" or "I will" statements?

    _____

    _____

    _____

12. I love remembering my beach trip with my friends Jessica and Ann and doing something so out of character: plunging into the ocean with a boogie board, surprising myself and my friends. Even getting my hair wet! It's one of my favorite rebellious acts of resilience because I remember how it made me laugh. I felt so light and free of some of the heaviness I'd been carrying.

    And fixing that ice maker! I am not a fix-it, handyman kind of girl, so I can't adequately explain to you what a victory this was to me. It made me feel brave and capable. It gave me back some of what I'd lost—confidence in myself. Confidence that I would be okay. Let's make a promise to ourselves: let's do at least one rebellious act of resilience per month.

Here are some ideas:

- Figure out how to do something you don't know how to do, big or small, and do it. Try not to give up if it's hard!
- Bring order to something you've been putting off. That closet? Your finances? The garage? If it feels overwhelming, make a list of each tiny step that will help you accomplish your goal and work on one step at a time.
- Try a new physical activity like Pilates or pickleball.
- Take a class and learn something new, such as a foreign language.
- Explore your creative side with a painting class or by learning to play a musical instrument.
- Create a boundary with someone who it's been hard to say no to. It doesn't have to be a big deal. "No, I can't serve on that committee. I am at capacity right now but thank you for asking." Or "No, I can't come over this Sunday. We really need some family time at home." Or maybe a bigger deal: "Because you won't stop texting me like I asked, I'm going to block your number."
- Plan a little or big trip to a favorite place or to a place you've never been.
- Plan an outing to somewhere nearby simply because it will make you happy. Again, small or big. You know I love playing cards, specifically Monopoly Deal. Going with friends to a new restaurant where we can sit, talk, eat, and play cards is one of my favorite simple outings.
- Do something a little adventurous—for you. It doesn't have to be bungee jumping! What is a little bit of an adventure just for you?

Make a list of some brave or adventurous or rebellious acts of resilience you might do. You don't have to do everything on your list right now, but dream big and have fun with this! Write your list here. And then also write it on a separate piece of paper where you can display it and be reminded of it.

_____

_____

_____

_____

_____

_____

_____

Then from that list, pick one thing you will do this week. Remember, do at least one per month! You might want to ask a friend to join you or hold you accountable.

13. "Over time, the more capable you feel, the more empowered you feel. The more empowered you feel, the more you'll trust your own discernment again. The more you trust your own discernment, the less you'll fear the risk of inviting the right imperfect people in. The less you'll resist trying to rebuild, rediscover, and remake your life that is so worth living. Really living. Not just barely making it through. But making your life better than it's ever been."

Which words stand out to you in this quote from the book?

_____

_____

_____

_____

_____

_____

_____

Action Steps

We've already explored some action steps in this chapter, specifically the rebellious acts of resilience in #12. If you haven't made your list, make that now. And if you haven't done at least one activity, can you do it today? This week? Don't forget to take pictures and add them to your Moving Forward folder.

Scripture

For the LORD will be your confidence, and will keep your foot from being caught.

PROVERBS 3:26 NASB

And we know that in all things God works for the good of those who love him, who have been called according to his purpose. For those God foreknew he also predestined to be conformed to the image of his Son, that he might be the firstborn among many brothers and sisters. And those he predestined, he also called; those he called, he also justified; those he justified, he also glorified.

What, then, shall we say in response to these things? If God is for us, who can be against us? He who did not spare his own Son, but gave him up for us all—how will he not also, along with him, graciously give us all things?

ROMANS 8:28–32

God is the one who began this good work in you, and I am certain that he won't stop before it is complete on the day that Christ Jesus returns.

PHILIPPIANS 1:6 CEV

Playlist

"For My Good," Maverick City Music, featuring Todd Galberth

"Praise You Anywhere," Brandon Lake

"This Is How I Thank the Lord," Mosaic MSC

Prayer

Dear Lord, sometimes jumping into the ocean feels exhilarating and exciting, while other times it feels scary and overwhelming. Just like moving forward in trust can feel. Today I want to focus on how I've healed and how I've grown in trust. Thank You for being with me every step of the way. Help me not to shrink back from the new or uncomfortable but to push through the unknown. Give me a heart to rejoice and to see where You are writing a promising new future for me. Amen.

Chapter 10

The Secret to Really Healing

I heard an old tale about a farmer with a life full of ups and downs. No matter what he was going through, his response to others when they commented "That's amazing" for the ups or "That's awful" for the downs was "We'll see."

He held the hard times with sadness and perspective but not with a clenched fist of bitterness and hopelessness. Saying "We'll see" doesn't diminish the good. But it does mean we can look at life through the lens of a continuous story rather than isolated instances.

And though we will face unkindness and unfaithfulness in people, hope is not lost because God is kind. God is faithful. When life begs me to believe otherwise, I remind myself that God's not done yet. There's more to be revealed. We'll see.

If I can't see it as I look forward, I look backward. The quicker I intentionally recall His faithfulness in my past, the less I panic and suffer from fear of the future. I'm learning how to step into—and sometimes fall into—uncertainty, while still whispering, "This is what it means to trust You, God."

I have learned that imperfect trust in His plan is still holy.

And though I still feel pricks of pain over some really hard stuff in the past, I'm so grateful I didn't stay stuck trying to make things happen my way and in my timing. At times in my stubbornness, I thought I knew what was best. It was God's grace all those times He told me no.

God helped me learn to lean on Him in the midst of my biggest disappointments and to sit alone and be okay. He helped me fight battles that are still going on, not with one great big miraculous intervention but instead with daily provisions and assurances.

And now I have the gift of seeing much more of how God protected me and provided for me because more time has passed. More of God's plans for me have unfolded. I have more perspective now.

As I write this journal it is 2024. When I saw those numbers written out for the first time this year, something in my heart clicked into place. *Wow*, I thought, *it's been ten years.* Ten years since things started happening in my first marriage that I didn't know about. So many years of things going from bad to worse to worse than I could ever imagine. No one but me and God will ever be able to understand the full magnitude of all that happened.

But I survived. And now, as I look back, I don't understand everything God allowed, but I see some of the reasons God took me through the darkest valleys. And I'm more confident than ever that He was right there with me every step of the way. So many things still don't make sense to me with my limited human thinking, but some crucial things do make sense.

Just this morning I had another epiphany about something God allowed that hurt deeply. I cried so many tears and shook my fist at God countless times over how unfair this circumstance seemed in real time. I begged God to make it different. I questioned His goodness and faithfulness. And so did some of my friends who were walking through it with me.

But I now see how God used that really awful circumstance to protect me in a big way. It reminds me of what I sometimes had to do with my children when they missed out on big things because I knew that telling them no was the best and wisest thing I could do as their parent. They couldn't understand the complexities of my reasons. They were never okay with the no. That is, until many years passed, and they now have their own children. Now they see why. And now they are grateful I stood my ground.

So it is with my relationship with God.

And I'm so grateful God stood His ground with me.

This morning I sat with a friend and prayed, thanking God for the very thing that made me question Him the most. What hurt in that moment was what helped me in the end. It's because God told me no that I am living the redemption I'm now in. Joel 2:25–26 in the New King James Version reads:

> "So I will restore to you the years that the swarming locust has eaten,
> The crawling locust,
> The consuming locust,
> And the chewing locust,
> My great army which I sent among you.
> You shall eat in plenty and be satisfied,
> And praise the name of the LORD your God,
> Who has dealt wondrously with you;
> And My people shall never be put to shame."

God has dealt wondrously with me. Yes, it took time. Yes, it took twists and turns and was full of setbacks from my perspective. Yes, it required me to soften my heart so I could see it. And yes, I know there are no guarantees for the future. So I'm not saying circumstances are and will forever be wonderful. No, what I'm saying is God has dealt with me wondrously. And today happens to be a day where my heart is celebrating where He led me after ten very long years.

The pages of my life have kept turning. My story continues to be written and so does yours. Whatever part of the journey you are in right now, remember, God's not done. We'll see.

My story continues to be written and so does yours. Whatever part of the journey you are in right now, remember, God's not done.

Guided Journaling

1. While on a hike, I saw a little plaque marking a fallen tree. The entire tree was lying on the ground, and the bottom part of the tree looked completely dead. The top of the tree, however, was not dead. Somehow, from this fallen position, the top branches continued to grow, with their green branches reaching skyward. The sign placed in front of the tree said, "The Resilient Oak Tree: The storm that felled this tree didn't stop it from protecting both the forest and island community with its thriving canopy."

    So many things about this tree spoke to me. I stood for a long time reflecting on it and imagining what kind of storms it must have taken to fell this tree. I imagined hurricanes and then storm after storm. But that tree held on. That tree continued to grow to the point where its leaves were thriving so much that it could provide a canopy. In other words, a shelter.

    For many, many years hurricane-force winds blew through my life. Life went from bad to worse before it ever got better. I wish it weren't true, but I know from talking to you that so many of you are also familiar with those long years where you wondered if you'd survive. Whether you've suffered the same level of broken trust as I did or a less severe level of broken trust, pain is pain, and we should never compare or minimize what we've been through.

    Do you have any thoughts about the storms that felled the tree? What does that lead you to think about the storms in your own life? About your own resiliency in those storms?

    _____

    _____

    _____

    _____

    _____

    _____

---

2. When I was betrayed, I walked a journey of being shocked to grief-stricken to numb to finally dealing with the pain of betrayal. I moved forward one step at a time, just like you. As I read the plaque and reflected on the tree, I thought, *What a beautiful legacy for a tree.*

   One word on the plaque that stood out to me was *community.* One of my struggles with betrayal is the ripple effects. It doesn't hurt just us; it hurts our community, our people. Children, other family members, friends, work, ministry. I found myself wanting to do anything I could to protect them from the consequences of what had been done to me. Have you also struggled with the far-reaching ripple effects of betrayal? Write about who's been affected, how that feels, and how you've handled it.

3. Another word that stood out to me was *canopy.* I picture the tree branches spreading wide and far, providing shade and protection for what and who are underneath. I tried to be the canopy, the protective covering, over those I loved who were affected by my situation, especially my kids. And many times, I was. Gradually, however, I realized that because God is sovereign, He had a reason for this being part of their story as well. He would be their canopy. Doing this released them to a place where they also would grow not in trusting me but in trusting God.

   Does that realization help you in your situation? Are there people you love who you need to surrender and allow God to be their canopy? Let's pray about that right now.

> *Heavenly Father, I really, really don't like how this situation has affected those I love. I still don't understand everything that You allowed to happen, but I've learned to trust You in it. And I want the same thing for my people. While I want to fix it and make it better and absorb all the hurt for them, I realize that is not my job. I surrender _____ (name of person or people) to You. Please help them to grow in trusting You in this situation. Amen.*

   Write down any thoughts you have about trusting God with the people you love.

---

4. One of the challenging things about any kind of hard situation is that the rest of life goes on. Our community often comes with responsibilities that don't go away. We still have to take care of kids and keep up with the daily life of cooking, cleaning up, laundry, errands, and everyday activities. We go to work and continue relationships. Maybe we can pull back on some duties but not all.

    Do you remember when I told you about my dream of running away to Montana in chapter 7? I wouldn't be surprised if there have been days you, too, wanted to run away. Or wanted to stay in bed. But you didn't. You carried on. Some days the only prayer you could come up with was "Jesus, I need You. That's all I got." But you still sought God, day after day.

    Can we stop for a minute and have a little celebration of *you*? Only you and God will know about some of the moments. And even if you think, *Yep, some days I did that and some days I fell apart*, you still did it. Write down something you are proud of and consider a victory in this season.

_____

_____

_____

_____

_____

_____

_____

_____

_____

_____

5. I discovered that maybe the secret to really healing is to change the end goal. Instead of expecting the healing work to return me to how I was before, I could let the healing make me into a healthier version of myself. Instead of focusing on all that was taken from me, maybe I could shift my focus to what this new season could give me.

Write about changing the end goal of your healing. What does that look like for you? What does the healthier version of you look like?

_____

_____

_____

_____

_____

_____

_____

_____

One of the biggest things that helps me heal is to share my story to encourage and help others. It's not super fun to have parts of my story I wish were different and to be vulnerable about those, especially when it's sometimes met with criticism and judgment. I've been writing and sharing for years, so it might seem that it's gotten easier. But it hasn't. Being vulnerable still feels risky. I sometimes feel myself wanting to pull back from sharing some of the more sensitive and tender places of my heart. I continue because I know it's what God wants me to do. He wants us to share whatever comfort we've received from Him with others. We read in 2 Corinthians 1:3–4, "All praise to God, the Father of our Lord Jesus Christ. God is our merciful Father and the source of all comfort. He comforts us in all our troubles so that we can comfort others. When they are troubled, we will be able to give them the same comfort God has given us" (NLT).

My greatest joy and sense of purpose comes when I share my pain and struggles, bringing them to the light of God's love and shining His love into the hearts of others. That is a moment that makes me think, *This is how God redeems our pain.*

Wisely, prayerfully, courageously open the door to your heart to someone who is struggling and dying inside with their hurt, not sure what to do with it, just like you were and still are sometimes. Maybe start small with one person . . . maybe more. Maybe open the door with words like, *I know how that feels too. I've been through the same thing.*

Have you already been open with someone about some of your struggles with trust? How did that go? How did it make you feel? If you haven't, pray about identifying that person and be willing to obey God however He leads you in this.

---

6. I never wanted to have the story of my life be that I'm the divorced Bible teacher. I never wanted to lose the friends I've lost. I never wanted to have people judge me, ridicule me, make up stories about me, or dismiss me as though divorce is emotional leprosy. But as I stood staring at that tree, I thought to myself, *They may have knocked me down. But I will accept what happened, grow some new roots, and turn broken into beautiful.*

What's your "I never . . ."? How do the words "broken into beautiful" inspire you concerning your trust journey? Write down some of the broken things that you can now see as beautiful.

7. The real antidote for trust issues isn't to perfectly choose the right people. It isn't to catch every rip and make sure it is repaired perfectly. The real solution is to accept that trust isn't a guarantee with humans—ever. Some relationships will hurt us. Some relationships will help heal us. But if we anchor our hope to the Lord, the risks of trust will be much less terrifying as we develop the muscles of resiliency.

Our lives have been altered but not ruined. We've been hurt, but we're choosing not to live hurt. We've pushed through resistance and fear to strengthen the relationships that are worthy of trust, and we've learned to create new trustworthy relationships.

One day we'll probably have our trust broken again—hopefully not in a huge way, but it will happen because that's simply life on this side of heaven. We won't respond the same way we did in the past, however, because we've changed, and we've seen the goodness of God. We've embraced this new season with better tools and fresh hope. And most importantly, we've anchored our trust to our trustworthy God. Ultimately, He's the antidote to trust issues.

It's a relief to me to realize that I don't have to be so vigilant to ensure I don't miss something and work so hard to repair everything perfectly. Yes, we've worked hard and been purposeful about moving forward, and that's a huge part of healing. But in the end when we partner with God in our growth, He will do the heavy lifting that we are not designed to do because we're designed to put our trust in Him.

How does believing God is the ultimate antidote to our trust issues change the way you think and live? Are you letting Him do the heavy lifting? Write about a person or situation you need to surrender to God.

_____

_____

_____

_____

_____

8. The woman who thrives in life isn't the one who never has her heart broken. It's the one who plants her brokenness in the rich soil of her faith in God and waits with anticipation to see what good thing God will grow next. Psalm 1:3 tells us, "That person is like a tree planted by streams of water, which yields its fruit in season and whose leaf does not wither—whatever they do prospers." Nothing we ever place in God's hands will be returned without meaning.

I remember reading this verse as a new Christian, and ever since then it's been a favorite. Its truth has been meaningful to me in so many situations, including trust issues. Even though I know we'll continue to encounter hard things concerning trust, we can still thrive. We can still yield fruit and display green leaves. How does this verse impact you? What does bearing fruit look like in you and your life as related to trust? What have you placed in God's hand that has become meaningful?

_____

_____

_____

_____

_____

_____

Action Steps

As a symbol and reminder of your healing journey, you might want to bury something and plant something. I'll let you use your creativity for this!

Add to and review your photos in your Moving Forward folder while playing songs from the playlist. You'll find a self-assessment right after this chapter. Don't skip it! We have so much growth and healing to celebrate!

Scripture

That person is like a tree planted by streams of water, which yields its fruit in season and whose leaf does not wither—whatever they do prospers.

PSALM 1:3

"So I will restore to you the years that the swarming locust has eaten, the crawling locust, the consuming locust, and the chewing locust, my great army which I sent among you. You shall eat in plenty and be satisfied, and praise the name of the Lord your God, who has dealt wondrously with you; and My people shall never be put to shame."

JOEL 2:25–26 NKJV

And the God of all grace, who called you to his eternal glory in Christ, after you have suffered a little while, will himself restore you and make you strong, firm and steadfast.

1 PETER 5:10

Playlist

"Great Is Thy Faithfulness," Carrie Underwood, featuring CeCe Winans

"How He Loves Us," Jesus Culture and Kim Walker-Smith

"Lost in Your Love," Brandon Lake, featuring Sarah Reeves

Prayer

Jesus, thank You for being with me in this journey of healing and moving forward. I see a difference in myself when it comes to trusting others, You, and myself. And that is something that feels so good. I want to remember this truth: There's not a person or situation more powerful than You. You are the Author of my story, and You write each page. I trust You with my story. Help me each day to stay surrendered to Your ways and to stay on our path. You lead; I'll follow. In Your name, amen.

Self-Assessment and Reflection

*D*on't skip this part! Take your time as you reflect on your trust journey. You'll discover places you still need to work on, but just as I asked you to be compassionate toward yourself at the beginning of the journal, I'll ask you to do the same now. Celebrate progress even if it's not perfect!

1. Let's think about the title, *I Want to Trust You, but I Don't: Moving Forward When You're Skeptical of Others, Afraid of What God Will Allow, and Doubtful of Your Own Discernment.* What do you think of when you read this title now? Where have you made progress and where do you want to continue to grow?

_____

_____

_____

_____

2. Complete this sentence in general or for how you feel about trusting others, God, and yourself: When it comes to trust, I feel . . .

_____

_____

_____

_____

_____

_____

_____

_____

_____

3. About trusting others, here's what I've learned that will help me:

_____

_____

_____

_____

_____

About trusting God, here's what I've learned that will help me:

_____

_____

_____

_____

About trusting myself, here's what I've learned that will help me:

_____

_____

_____

_____

4. As you've progressed through this journal, you've changed. Let's look at the words on the left as the way you were at the beginning of this journey. Now look at the words on the right as representing ways you've grown in trust. It doesn't mean that you've mastered trust perfectly; it simply illustrates progress. Draw a line from a word on the left to a word on the right to show the ways you've grown in trust.

anxious	hopeful
self-protective	peaceful
skeptical	eager
afraid	secure
regretful	happy
ashamed	content
angry	joyful
cautious	calm
sad	open
doubtful	confident
hopeless	steady
unsure	safe

Respond to the following:

5. One of the main ways I've healed my trust issues is . . .

6. A significant way I've changed when it comes to trust is . . .

7. I still fear _____ when it comes to trust.

8. I still get sad . . .

9. I know I can trust this person . . .

10. Today I am celebrating moving forward in trust in these ways . . .

11. I am using my voice more when . . .

12. I've become more confident in myself about . . .

_____

_____

_____

_____

_____

13. I've taken baby steps . . .

_____

_____

_____

_____

_____

14. I've taken big steps . . .

_____

_____

_____

_____

_____

15. I'm proud of myself . . .

_____

_____

_____

_____

16. I'm thankful . . .

_____

_____

_____

_____

_____

17. I've forgiven . . .

_____

_____

_____

_____

_____

18. I've surrendered . . .

_____

_____

_____

_____

_____

19. The thing about trust that's become easier is . . .

_____

_____

_____

20. Concerning this journey of growing in trust, I'm thankful to God for . . .

_____

_____

_____

_____

_____

21. Do one or all of the following to reflect on your journey forward in trust:

A. Write a letter to yourself and one to Jesus. In the letters reflect on how you've changed in terms of trusting others, God, and yourself. You might want to include thoughts on the following:

- Your outlook about the future
- Triggers and how you deal with them
- Recognizing red flags
- Speaking up
- Repairing rips
- Knowing when to keep trying or when to let go
- Putting healthy boundaries into place
- Being alone
- Moving forward in relationships
- Fear of what-ifs
- Surrendering
- Baby steps forward
- Big leaps forward
- Attaching hope to God alone
- Being brave
- Letting go of fears
- Letting God work out justice
- Recognizing that some questions may never be answered

- Rebellious acts of resilience
- Trusting others
- Trusting God
- Trusting yourself
- Forgiving
- Sharing with others what you've learned

B. Draw a map of the journey of growing in trust from where you were at the beginning of journaling to where you are now.

C. Sing a song, dance a dance, write a poem, or make a digital or paper collage to depict your journey of growing in trust. Do something to celebrate!

A Closing Note from Lysa

*F*riend, I'm so glad you joined me on this journey of moving forward
with a better understanding of trust and distrust. You are stronger than you know.
You are wiser than you sometimes give yourself credit for. You are more alive today
than ever before. Now, when it is wise, dare to trust again. Do it carefully, applying what
you've learned. But don't put the pressure on yourself to do this trust thing perfectly. God will
be right there with you. And, as we've learned together, no one is more powerful than God.

Some of your people will be trustworthy, and some will not. But you, my friend, are
now well prepared to do the best you can and keep on walking. And the next time we
bump into each other, I hope we both have stories of relationships with loved ones that
are safe, healthy, and much more peaceful, and that we are able to wisely and confidently
tell the right people, "I want to trust you, and now I do."

Getting the Help You Need

Dear friend,

For some of you this book will be exactly what you needed to help you handle broken trust and navigate your healing when this happens. For some this book might be a guide for repairing trust that's been damaged. But for others this book might help you see that distrust is actually the wisest choice you can make. Because I'm not a licensed counselor and this book doesn't take the place of therapy, please know there are some difficult realities in life that you will want a licensed Christian counselor to help you navigate. Please be honest about your need for counseling help. I am so thankful for the professionals who have lovingly helped lead me through my darkest days. It's always been important to me that the professional counselors I've seen have a deeply committed personal relationship with Jesus and understand the battle must be fought in both the physical and spiritual realm. A great resource to find a Christian counselor in your area is the American Association of Christian Counselors at aacc.net. With counselors in all fifty states, their heart is to connect people who hurt with people who help.

I'm praying for you, dear friend.
Much love,

Some Important Notes to Consider on Abuse

A couple of times throughout this book, I've referenced not excusing away abuse or dysfunctional behavior. You know from reading so much about my personal experiences, my heart is very tender and compassionate toward anyone facing destructive relational realities. I wanted to provide this information, both as a point of compassion and clarity around what abuse is and as a way to potentially find help if you're in an abusive situation.

In an article published by Psychology Today, I found this definition of abuse:

Abuse within families is behaviorally nuanced and emotionally complex. Always, it is within a dynamic of power and control that emotional and physical abuse is perpetuated.

Abuse may manifest as physical (*throwing, shoving, grabbing, blocking pathways, slapping, hitting, scratches, bruises, burns, cuts, wounds, broken bones, fractures, damage to organs, permanent injury, or even murder*), sexual (*suggestive flirtatiousness, propositioning, undesired or inappropriate holding, kissing, fondling of sexual parts, oral sex, or any kind of forceful sexual activity*), or emotional (*neglect, harassment, shaming, threatening, malicious tricks, blackmail, unfair punishments, cruel or degrading tasks, confinement, abandonment*).[4]

So, what does the Bible say about abuse, and what do we do about it? Let's look at what Paul wrote to Timothy:

But understand this, that in the last days there will come times of difficulty. For people will be lovers of self, lovers of money, proud, arrogant, abusive, disobedient to their parents, ungrateful, unholy, heartless, unappeasable, slanderous, without self-control, brutal, not loving good, treacherous, reckless, swollen with conceit, lovers of pleasure rather than lovers of God, having the appearance of godliness, but denying its power. Avoid such people. (2 Timothy 3:1–5 esv)

I'm thankful for verses like these that clearly state to avoid abusive people. But how to avoid them and exactly how this is carried out is so very complex. It's impossible to put a broad, sweeping formula on top of hard relationships. There are so many factors that must be sorted out with people trained to recognize danger and to help lead those in abusive situations to know what to do and how to do it.

Here are some things to consider:

- It is good to have wise people speaking into our lives and to process life concerns with godly mentors and trusted friends. Here's a good verse to help discern people of wisdom in your life:

  Who is wise and understanding among you? By his good conduct let him show his works in the meekness of wisdom. But if you have bitter jealousy and selfish ambition in your hearts, do not boast and be false to the truth. This is not the wisdom that comes down from above, but is earthly, unspiritual, demonic. For where jealousy and selfish ambition exist, there will be disorder and every vile practice. But the wisdom from above is first pure, then peaceable, gentle, open to reason, full of mercy and good fruits, impartial and sincere. And a harvest of righteousness is sown in peace by those who make peace. (James 3:13–18 esv)

- These trusted friends and godly mentors speaking wisdom into our lives can help us recognize behaviors that cross the line and should be brought to the attention of a professional counselor educated on the issues at hand or, in more urgent situations, to the attention of authorities.

If you need to find a professional Christian counselor in your area, both Focus on the Family and the American Association of Christian Counselors have recommendations listed on their websites, or your church may also have a list of trusted Christian counselors they recommend.

Please know, friend, you are loved, you are not alone, and you don't have to walk through this without help. Remember, the person who is hurting you needs help that only trained professionals can give them. Getting the proper authorities involved isn't being unloving . . . it's actually for your safety and theirs.

Notes

1. *Merriam-Webster*, s.v. "hope (*v.*)," accessed July 8, 2024, https://www.merriam-webster.com/dictionary/hope.
2. Maya Angelou, on *The Oprah Winfrey Show*, aired June 18, 1997, Oprah Winfrey Network, https://www.oprah.com/own-oprahshow/one-of-dr-maya-angelous-most-important-lessons_1.
3. Simone Marie, "Can You Get 'Stuck' at the Age You Experienced Trauma?" PsychCentral, Healthline Media, updated January 5, 2022, https://psychcentral.com/ptsd/signs-trauma-has-you-stuck.
4. Blake Griffin Edwards, "Secret Dynamics of Emotional, Sexual, and Physical Abuse," *Psychology Today*, Sussex Publishers, LLC, February 23, 2019, https://www.psychologytoday.com/us/blog/progress-notes/201902/secret-dynamics-emotional-sexual-and-physical-abuse.

About the Author

Lysa TerKeurst Adams is president and chief visionary officer of Proverbs 31 Ministries and the author of seven *New York Times* bestsellers, including *Good Boundaries and Goodbyes*, *Forgiving What You Can't Forget*, and *It's Not Supposed to Be This Way*. She enjoys life with her husband, Chaz, and her kids and grandkids. Connect with her at www.LysaTerKeurst.com or on social media @LysaTerKeurst.

The *Therapy & Theology* Podcast

Where Lysa TerKeurst, Dr. Joel Muddamalle, and Licensed Professional Counselor Jim Cress help you work through what you're walking through.

If you ever had questions about topics like:

Boundaries ...
Narcissism ...
Trust Issues ...
Addiction ...

You'll get the scriptural wisdom and the therapeutic insights you need.

THERAPYANDTHEOLOGYPODCAST.COM